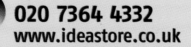

Library Learning Information

Idea Store®
Whitechapel
321 Whitechapel Road
London E1 1BU

020 7364 4332
www.ideastore.co.uk

Created and managed by
Tower Hamlets Council

Hatred of Democracy

Hatred of Democracy

JACQUES RANCIÈRE

Translated by Steve Corcoran

VERSO

London • New York

This edition published by Verso 2006
© Verso 2006
Translation © Steve Corcoran 2006
First published as *La haine de la démocratie*
© La Fabrique 2005

1 3 5 7 9 10 8 6 4 2

Verso
UK: 6 Meard Street, London W1F 0EG
USA: 180 Varick Street, New York, NY 10014-4606
www.versobooks.com

Verso is the imprint of New Left Books

ISBN-13: 978-1-84467-098-7
ISBN-10: 1-84467-098-8

British Library Cataloguing in Publication Data
A catalogue record for this book is available from the British
Library

Library of Congress Cataloging-in-Publication Data
A catalog record for this book is available from the Library of
Congress

Typeset in Times by Hewer Text UK Ltd
Printed in the USA by Quebecor World

Contents

Introduction

A young woman keeps France in suspense with her story of a make-believe attack;[1] a few adolescents refuse to take their headscarves off at school; social security is running a deficit; Montesquieu, Voltaire and Baudelaire dethrone Racine and Corneille as texts presented at the baccalaureate; wage earners hold demonstrations to defend their retirement schemes; a Grande École creates an alternative entrance scheme;[2] reality TV, homosexual marriage and artificial insemination increase in popularity. There is no point looking for what groups together events of such disparate natures. Book after book, article after article, programme after programme, hundreds of philosophers and sociologists, political scientists and psycho-analysts, journalists and writers, have already supplied us with the response. All these symptoms, they say, are manifestations of the same illness; for all these effects there is only one cause. This cause is called democracy, that is, the reign of the limitless desire of individuals in modern mass society.

It is imperative to see what constitutes the singularity of this denunciation. Hatred of democracy is certainly nothing new. Indeed it is as old as democracy itself for a simple reason: the word itself is an expression of hatred. It was, in Ancient Greece, originally used as an insult by those who saw in the unnameable government of the multitude the ruin of any legitimate order. It remained synonymous with abomination for everyone who thought that power fell by rights to those whose birth had predestined them to it or whose capabilities called them to it. And it still is today for those who construe revelations of divine law as the sole legitimate foundation on which to organize human communities. The violence of this hatred is certainly on the contemporary agenda. It is not, though, an objective of this book, for a simple reason: I have nothing in common with those that spread it, and so nothing to discuss with them.

Alongside this hatred of democracy, history has born witness to the forms of its critique. Critique acknowledges something's existence, but in order to confine it within limits. There have been two great historical forms of critique of democracy. There was the art of aristocratic legislators and experts who strove to make a compromise with democracy, viewed as a fact that could not be ignored. The drawing up of the United States constitution is the classic example of this work of composing forces and of balancing institutional mechanisms intended to get the most possible out of the fact of democracy, all the while strictly containing it in order to protect two goods taken as synonymous: the government of the best, and the preservation of the order of property. The success of that *critique en acte* naturally fuelled the success of its contrary. The young Marx had no troubles exposing the reign of property lying at the foundation of the republican constitution. The republican legislators had made no secret of it. But in so doing he was able to set a standard of thought whose resources have not yet been exhausted: the notion that the laws and institutions of formal democracy are appearances under which, and instruments by which, the power of the bourgeois class is exercised. The struggle against appearances thus became the path leading to 'real' democracy, where liberty and equality would no longer be represented in the institutions of law and State but embodied in the very forms of concrete life and sensible experience.

The new hatred of democracy that is the subject of this book does not strictly fall under either of these models, though it combines elements borrowed from both. Its spokespersons all live in countries that proclaim themselves to be not just democratic States but democracies *tout court*. None of them call for a democracy that would be more real. On the contrary, they have all had too much of it. Though they don't complain about the institutions professing to embody the power of the people, nor do they propose any measures to restrain that power. The institutional mechanics that impassioned the contemporaries of Montesquieu, Madison and Tocqueville do not interest them. It is about the people and its mores that they complain, not about the institutions of its power. For them democracy is not a corrupt form of government; it is a crisis of civilization afflicting society and through it the State. Whence, some movement back and forth that might at first sight seem surprising. Indeed, the same critics who endlessly denounce that democratic America for having given us all the evils associated with the respect for differences, minority rights and affirmative action, that undermine [French] republican universalism, are the first to applaud when the same America undertakes to spread its democracy throughout the world with armed force.

Double discourse on democracy is certainly nothing new. We are accustomed to hearing that democracy is the worst of governments with the exception of all the others. But the new antidemocratic sentiment gives the general formula a more troubling expression. Democratic government, it says, is bad when it is allowed to be corrupted by democratic society, which wants for everyone to be equal and for all differences to be respected. It is good, on the other hand, when it rallies individuals enfeebled by democratic society to the vitality of war in order to defend the values of civilization, the values pertaining to the clash of civilizations. The thesis of the new hatred of democracy can be succinctly put: there is only one good democracy, the one that represses the catastrophe of democratic civilization. The pages that follow will try to analyze the formation of this thesis and draw out its stakes. The issue is not simply to describe a form of contemporary ideology. For this analysis will also inform us about the state of our world and about what this world understands by politics. Accordingly, it can help us positively to understand the scandal borne by the word democracy and to rediscover the trenchancy of its idea.

1

From Victorious Democracy
to Criminal Democracy

'Democracy Stirs In The Middle East': with this title a
magazine that carries the flame of economic neoliberalism
celebrated some months ago the success of the elections in
Iraq and the anti-Syrian demonstrations in Beirut.[3] Only this
praise of victorious democracy was accompanied by commentaries specifying the nature and limits of this democracy.
Democracy triumphed, we were told, despite protests by
idealists for whom democracy consists in the government
of the people by the people, and so cannot be brought to a
people by the force of arms. Hence, it triumphed when seen
from a realistic point of view, that is, one that separates out
the practical benefits from the utopia of the government of
the people by the people. But the lesson addressed to the
idealists also urged us to be consistent in our realism.
Democracy has triumphed, but one must understand the
meaning of this triumph: bringing democracy to another
people does not simply mean bringing it the beneficial effects

of a constitutional State, elections and a free press. It also means bringing it disorder.

One will recall the statement issued by the American Secretary of Defense concerning the pillaging that occurred after the fall of Saddam Hussein. We have, he basically said, brought freedom to the Iraqis. And yet, freedom also means the freedom to do wrong. This statement is not merely a circumstantial witticism. It is part of a broader logic that can be reconstituted from its disjoined elements: it is because democracy is not the idyll of the government of the people by the people, but the disorder of passions eager for satisfaction, that it can, and even must, be introduced from outside by the armed might of a superpower, meaning not only a State disposing of disproportionate military power, but more generally the power to master democratic disorder.

The commentaries attending these expeditions devoted to spreading democracy throughout the world remind us then of older arguments which (but in a far less triumphal tone) invoked democracy's irresistible expansion. In effect, they merely paraphrase the accounts that were presented thirty years ago at the Trilateral Commission, pointing up what was then called the crisis of democracy.[4]

Democracy stirs in the wake of American armies, in spite of those idealists who protest in the name of peoples' rights to self-determination. Thirty years ago, the aforementioned report accused the same kind of idealists – those 'value-oriented intellectuals' who fuel a culture of opposition and an excess of democratic activity – of being as disastrous to the authority of the public interest [*la chose publique*] as they were to the pragmatic actions of those 'policy-oriented intellectuals'. Democracy stirs, but disorder stirs with it; the looters in Baghdad, who took advantage of their new democratic freedoms to procure more personal belongings at the expense of common property, evoked, in their slightly primitive manner, one of the major arguments that was used thirty years ago to demonstrate the 'crisis' of democracy: democracy, said the report writers, signifies the irresistible growth of demands that put pressure on governments, lead to a decline in authority, and cause individuals and groups to become refractory to the discipline and sacrifices required for the common good.

As such, the arguments used to back up the military campaigns devoted to the worldwide rise of democracy reveal the paradox concealed by the dominant usage of the word today. In these arguments democracy would appear to have two adversaries. On the one hand, it is opposed to a clearly identified enemy – arbitrary government, government without limits – which, depending on the moment, is referred to either as tyranny, dictatorship, or totalitarianism. But this self-evident opposition conceals another, more intimate, one. A good democratic government is one capable of controlling the evil quite simply called democratic life.

Such was the demonstration developed throughout *The Crisis of Democracy*: what provokes the crisis is nothing other than the intensity of democratic life. But this intensity and its subsequent danger have two facets: on the one hand, 'democratic life' would seem to be identical to the 'anarchic' principle that affirms the power of the people, whose extreme consequences the United States and other Western States experienced throughout the 1960s and 1970s: persistent militant contestation in all domains of State activity; undermining of the principles of good government, of the respect for public authorities, of the knowledge of experts, and of the know-how of pragmatists.

The remedy for this excess of democratic vitality has, if we can take Aristotle's word for it, been known since Pisistratus.[5]

It consists in redirecting the feverish energy activated on the public stage toward other ends, in sending it on a search for material prosperity, private happiness and social bonds. Alas! the right solution immediately revealed its flipside: diminishing excessive political energy, and promoting the quest for individual happiness and social relations, meant promoting a vitality of private life and forms of social interaction that led to heightened expectations and escalating demands. And these, of course, had in turn a twofold effect: they rendered citizens insouciant to the public good and undermined the authority of governments summoned to respond to the spiralling demands emanating from society.

So, confronting democratic vitality took the form of a double bind that can be succinctly put: either democratic life signified a large amount of popular participation in discussing public affairs, and it was a bad thing; or it stood for a form of social life that turned energies toward individual satisfaction, and it was a bad thing. Hence, good democracy must be that form of government and social life capable of controlling the double excess of collective activity and individual withdrawal inherent to democratic life.

Such is the standard form by which experts state the democratic paradox: as a social and political form of life, democracy is the reign of excess. This excess signifies the ruin of democratic government and must therefore be repressed by it. This squaring of the circle would once have excited the ingenuity of constitutional artists. But such an art is no longer highly thought of today. Governments get on perfectly well without it. For them, the fact that democracies are 'ungovernable' is abundant proof of the need they have to be governed, and that is all the legitimation they need for the care they put into governing them. But the virtues of governmental empiricism are hardly capable of convincing anyone except those who govern. Intellectuals have need of other fare, especially on this side of the Atlantic, and especially in France, where they are at once at one remove from power and excluded from its exercise. For them an empirical paradox cannot be dealt with by the arms of governmental bricolage. They see in it a consequence of some original vice, some perversion at the very heart of civilization, and they apply themselves to tracking down its principle. For them, then, the aim is to unravel the ambiguity of a name, to make 'democracy' no longer the common name of an evil and the good that cures it, but the sole name for an evil that corrupts us all.

While the American army was working toward democratic expansion in Iraq, a book was published in France that put the question of democracy in the Middle East under a wholly different light. It was called *Les Penchants criminels de l'Europe démocratique* [The Criminal Inclinations of Democratic Europe]. In it the author, Jean-Claude Milner,[6] developed, in a subtle and condensed analysis, a thesis as simple as it is radical. The present crime of European democracy is that it calls for peace in the Middle East, in other words, for a peaceful solution to the Israeli–Palestinian conflict. Such a peace could mean only one thing, the destruction of Israel. European democracies have pushed for peace between the conflicting sides to resolve the Israeli problem. However, European democratic peace itself was the result of nothing less than the extermination of the European Jews. A Europe unified in peace and democracy was rendered possible after 1945 for a single reason: because, due to the Nazi genocide's success, the European territory found itself rid of the people that formed the obstacle to realizing its dream, namely, the Jews. A Europe without borders means in effect dissolving politics, which always concerns limited totalities, into that society whose principle is on the contrary limitlessness. Modern democracy signifies the destruction of political limits by means of the law of limitlessness proper to modern society. This will to go beyond all limits is at once served and exemplified by that modern invention par excellence, technology. It culminates today in the desire to do away, by means of genetic manipulation and artificial insemination, with the very laws of sexual reproduction and affiliation. European democracy is the mode of society that bears that desire. In order to achieve its goal, according to Milner, it had to get rid of the people for whom the principle of existence itself is that of kinship and transmission, the people bearing the name that points to this principle, that is the people bearing the name of Jew. Such is precisely, he says, what the genocide brought Europe, thanks to an invention homogeneous to the principle of democratic society, the technical invention of the gas chamber. Democratic Europe, he concludes, is born in genocide, and it pursues the task in its desire to subject the Jewish State to the conditions it lays down for peace, conditions for the extermination of the Jews.

There are many ways to consider this argumentation. One can oppose to its radicality the rationality of common sense and of historical accuracy by asking, for example, if it is really so very easy, without recourse to a ruse of reason or a providential teleology of history, to conceive the Nazi regime as an agent of the triumph of European democracy. Conversely, one can analyse its internal coherence by interrogating the core of the author's thought, being a theory of the name that is articulated on the Lacanian triad of the symbolic, the imaginary and the real.[7] I shall take a third path: one that consists in probing the kernel of the argument not according to its extravagance with regard to common sense nor its conformity to the conceptual network of the author's thought, but from the point of view of the common landscape that this singular argument enables us to reconstitute, from what it allows us to perceive of the displacement that the term democracy has, in two decades, undergone within dominant intellectual opinion.

This displacement is recapitulated in Milner's book through the conjunction of two theses: the first radically opposes the name of Jew to that of democracy; the second turns that opposition into a divide between two humanities: on the one hand, a humanity faithful to the principle of kinship; on the other, a humanity forgetful of that principle in its pursuit of the ideal of self-generation, which is just as much an ideal of self-destruction. The Jew and democracy are in radical opposition. This thesis marks the overturning that has occurred of what structured the dominant perception of democracy at the time of the Six-Day War and the Sinai War. At that time, Israel was paid tribute for being a democracy. It was held up as a society that was governed by a State assuring both individual freedom and the participation of the greatest number in public life. The Declaration of Human Rights was viewed as the charter that epitomized this delicate balancing of the collectivity and guarantees of individual freedom. The contrary of democracy at the time was referred to as totalitarianism. The dominant discourse designated States as totalitarian if, in the name of the power of the collective, they denied both individuals' rights and constitutional forms of collective expression: free elections, and the freedom of expression and association. The term totalitarianism was reserved for designating the principle of that twofold denial. A total State was a State that suppressed the duality of State and society, extending the sphere of its exercise to the totality of collective life. Nazism and Communism were construed as the two paradigms of totalitarianism, founded on notions that claimed to transcend any separation between State and society, those of race and of class respectively. The Nazi State was considered, then, from the point of view it had itself proclaimed, that of being a State founded on race. Hence, the genocide of the Jews was regarded as the realization of the desire this State proclaimed to eliminate a race seen as degenerate and as bearing degeneracy.

Milner's book proposes the exact reversal of this once dominant belief: henceforth the virtue of Israel is that it signifies the contrary of the principle of democracy; the concept of totalitarianism is divested of any use; and the Nazi regime and its politics of any specificity. There is a very simple reason for this: the properties that were formerly attributed to totalitarianism, conceived as the State devouring society, have quite simply become the properties of democracy, conceived as society devouring the State. If Hitler, whose major concern was not to spread democracy, can be seen as the providential agent of that expansion, this is because what the antidemocrats of today refer to as democracy is the same thing that yesterday's zealots of 'liberal democracy' referred to as totalitarianism: the same thing turned upside down. What was only recently denounced as the State principle of a closed totality is now denounced as the social principle of limitlessness. This principle called democracy has become the englobing principle of modernity viewed as an historical and global totality to which the sole name of Jew stands in opposition as the principle of maintaining the human tradition. The American thinker of the 'crisis of democracy' might still oppose (as pertinent to the 'clash of civilizations') Western and Christian democracy to an Islam synonymous with the despotic Orient.[8] The French thinker of democratic crime, for his part, proposes a radicalized version of the war of civilizations, opposing democracy, Christianity and Islam, all merged together, to the sole Jewish exception.

We can, then, in a first analysis, circle in on the principle of this new antidemocratic discourse. The portrait it traces of democracy comprises traits that until quite recently were attributed to totalitarianism. Drawing up this portrait, then, implies a process of disfiguration: as if the concept of totalitarianism, forged for the purpose of the Cold War, and having lost its function, can be disassembled and its traits recomposed to remake the portrait of democracy, i.e., the thing that was its alleged contrary. We can reconstruct the stages of this process of defiguration and recomposition. It began at the start of the 1980s with a first operation that called into question the two sides of the opposition. The terrain on which this operation was played out was that of the reconsideration of the revolutionary heritage of democracy. The role played by François Furet's work *Interpreting the French Revolution*, published in 1978, has often been underlined. But the double thrust of the operation he performed has scarcely been noticed. To put the Terror again at the heart of the democratic revolution amounted, at the most visible level, to breaking the opposition that had structured the dominant opposition. Totalitarianism and democracy, Furet taught us, are not really opposed. The reign of Stalinist terror was already anticipated in the reign of revolutionary terror. And further, revolutionary terror had not at all derailed the Revolution; it was consubstantial with its project – it was a necessity inherent to the very essence of the democratic revolution.

Deducing Stalinist terror from French revolutionary terror was not in itself a new thing. This analysis had already been integrated into the classic opposition pitting liberal parliamentary democracy against a radical egalitarian democracy that sacrificed the rights of individuals to the religion of the collective and the blind fury of the hordes. A renewed denunciation of terrorist democracy seemed, then, to entail conceiving a new basis for a pragmatic and liberal democracy finally delivered from the revolutionary fantasies of the collective body.

But this simple reading omits the double thrust of the operation. For the critique of the Terror has a twofold basis. The critique known as liberal – which arraigns the totalitarian rigours of equality before the wise republic of individual liberties and parliamentary representation – was from the beginning subordinated to a totally different critique, one for which the sin of the revolution was not its collectivism, but, on the contrary, its individualism. On this view, the French Revolution was terroristic not for having refused to recognize the rights of individuals; it was terroristic for having consecrated them. Initiated by the theoreticians of the counter-revolution in the wake of the French Revolution, relayed by utopian socialists in the first half of the nineteenth century, consecrated at the end of the same century by the young science of sociology, this first reading can be stated as follows: the Revolution was the consequence of Enlightenment thinking and of its first principle – the 'Protestant' doctrine that elevates the judgement of isolated individuals to the level of structures and collective beliefs. Shattering the old solidarities that the monarchy, the nobility and the Church had slowly woven, the Protestant revolution dissolved the social link and atomized individuals. The Terror was the rigorous consequence of this dissolution and of the will to recreate, by the artifice of institutions and laws, a link that only natural and historical solidarities can weave.

It was this doctrine that was once again given the place of honour in Furet's book. Revolutionary terror, he showed, was consubstantial with the Revolution itself, since the revolutionary theatre in its entirety was founded on an ignorance of the profound historical realities that rendered it possible. It ignored the fact that the true revolution, that of institutions and moral values, had already taken place in the depths of society and in the cogs of the monarchical machine. The Revolution, henceforth, could no longer be anything but the illusion of starting from scratch – at a conscious level – the revolution that had already been accomplished. It could be nothing but the artifice of Terror striving to give an imaginary body to a society that had come undone. As evidence, Furet's account deferred to the theses of Claude Lefort which postulate the notion that democracy is a disembodied power.[9] But it put its trust still further in the work that furnished it with the materials of its reasoning, namely Augustin Cochin's thesis denouncing the role played by the '*sociétés de pensée*' in the origins of the French Revolution.[10] Augustin Cochin, Furet emphasized, was not just a royalist partisan of *Action française*, he was someone who had been nourished on Durkheimian sociological science. Indeed, he was the true legatee of the critique of 'individualist' revolution that had been transmitted by the counter-revolution to 'liberal' thinking and to republican sociology, and which forms the real basis of the denunciations of revolutionary 'totalitarianism'. The liberalism displayed by the French intelligentsia since the 1980s is a doctrine with a double thrust. Behind its reverence for the Enlightenment, and for the Anglo-American tradition of liberal democracy and human rights, one can discern a very French denunciation of the individualist revolution tearing apart the social body.

This double thrust of the critique of revolution enables us to understand the formation of contemporary antidemocratism. It enables us to understand the inversion in discourse on democracy consecutive to the collapse of the Soviet Empire. On the one hand, the fall of this Empire was, for a somewhat brief time, welcomed as the victory of democracy over totalitarianism, as the victory of individual liberty over State oppression, symbolized by those human rights that the Soviet dissidents and the Polish workers had been appealing to. These 'formal' rights were themselves the principal target of Marxist critique, so the collapse of the very regime built on the claim to be advancing 'real democracy' seemed to signal their revenge. But behind the obligatory salute to victorious human rights and a rediscovered democracy, the exact opposite happened. As soon as the concept of totalitarianism was no longer of use, the opposition between the good democracy of human rights and individual liberties, and the bad collectivist and egalitarian democracy, also fell into disuse. The critique of human rights immediately reasserted itself. Some construed it in the manner of Hannah Arendt: human rights are an illusion because they are the rights of that bare humanity that is without rights. Such rights are the illusory rights of a humanity that has been chased away from its homes and country, and away from citizenship altogether, by tyrannical regimes. It is well known that this account has made something of a comeback in recent times. On the one hand, it has opportunely come back to lend support to those liberating, humanitarian campaigns of States which, on behalf of militarist and militant democracy, assume the responsibility of defending the rights of those without rights. On the other hand, it has inspired Giorgio Agamben's account according to which the 'state of exception' is the real content of our democracy.[11] But the critique could also be construed in the manner of a certain Marxism that both the Soviet Empire's fall, and the weakening of movements of emancipation in the West, once more made available for all intents and purposes: human rights are the rights of egotistical individuals of bourgeois society.

The crucial thing is knowing just who these individuals are. For Marx they were the possessors of the means of production, i.e., the dominant class of which the State of human rights was the instrument. Contemporary wisdom views things differently. In fact, a series of tiny shifts is all that it is required to give egotistical individuals a completely different face. For a start, let's replace 'egotistical individuals' with 'greedy consumers', something which will hardly be denied. Then, let's suppose that the greedy consumers are a socio-historical species called 'democratic man'. Lastly, let's not forget that democracy is the regime of equality and we can conclude: the egotistical individuals are none other than those democratic men and women; and the generalization of commodity relations, of which the Rights of Man are emblematic, is basically nothing other than the realization of the feverish demand for equality that gets democratic individuals fired up and ruins the search for the common good embodied in the State.

Let's listen, for example, to the music of these sentences describing the sad state into which we have fallen thanks to what the author calls providential democracy:

> The relationship between physician and patient, lawyer and client, priest and parishioner, professor and student, and social worker and 'assisted' citizen increasingly conforms to the model of contractual relationships between equal individuals (or equal parties); that is, to a fundamentally egalitarian relationship model that is established between a provider of services and his client. *Homo*

democraticus becomes impatient whenever faced with competence, including that of a physician or lawyer. Competence calls into question his own sovereignty. Relationships that he maintains with others lose their political or metaphysical horizons. All professional practices tend to become trivialized in this sense . . . Doctors are gradually becoming salaried employees of the Social Security system; priests are becoming social workers and providers of sacraments . . . This is because the sacred dimension – made up of religious belief, situations of life and death, humanist or political values – is diminishing. The professions that gave an even indirect or modest shape to collective values, and thereby instituted them, are affected by the erosion of collective transcendence, be it religious or political.[12]

This long-winded moan purports to be describing the state of a world that democratic man has fashioned in his various guises: an impassive consumer of medication or sacraments; a trade unionist wanting ever more from the welfare state; a representative of ethnic minorities demanding recognition of their identity; a feminist campaigning for quotas; a student treating school as a supermarket where the client is king. But obviously the music of these sentences that claim to be describing the state of the everyday world in our times of hypermarkets and reality TV is an echo from way back. This 'description' of our everyday life in the year 2002 was already written down *tel quel* 150 years ago in the pages of the *Communist Manifesto*: the bourgeoisie

has drowned the most heavenly ecstasies of religious fervour, of chivalrous enthusiasm, of philistine sentimentalism, in the icy water of egotistical calculation. It has resolved personal worth into exchange value, and in place of the numberless indefeasible

chartered freedoms, has set up that single unconscionable freedom
– Free Trade . . . The bourgeoisie has stripped of its halo every
occupation hitherto honoured and looked up to with reverent awe.
It has converted the physician, the lawyer, the priest, the poet, the
man of science into its paid wage labourers.

The description of phenomena is the same. What contemporary sociology has contributed of its own accord is not new facts, but a new interpretation. It claims that the set of these facts has a sole cause: the impatience of democratic man who approaches every relation on one and the same model, i.e., 'the fundamentally egalitarian relations that obtain between a service provider and his or her client'.[13] The original text said the following: that the bourgeoisie has, 'in place of the numberless indefeasible chartered freedoms, set up that single unconscionable freedom – Free Trade'; and that the only equality it knows is commercial equality, based on brutal and shameless exploitation, on a fundamental inequality in relations between the service 'providers' of work and the 'clients' who buy their labour power. The modified text replaces the 'bourgeoisie' with another subject, 'democratic man'. From this point it then becomes possible to transform the reign of exploitation into the reign of equality, and, without further ceremony, to make democratic equality identical to the 'equal exchange' of market services. Marx's text, revised and corrected, says in a word: the equality of human rights expresses the 'equality' of the relations of exploitation, which is tantamount to accomplishing the ideals of which democratic man dreams.

The equation democracy = limitlessness = society, on which the denunciation of the 'crimes' of democracy is based, presupposes, then, a threefold operation: it is imperative, first, to reduce democracy to a form of society; second, to make this form of society identical to the reign of the egalitarian individual by grouping under the latter all sorts of disparate properties, everything from mass consumption to the claims of special minority rights, not to forget union battles; and finally, to charge 'mass individualist society', henceforth identical to democracy, with pursuing the limitless growth that is inherent to the logic of the capitalist economy.

This collapsing of the political, the sociological and the economic into one plane frequently claims to be following in the footsteps of Tocqueville's conception of democracy as the equality of conditions. But such a claim itself presupposes a very simplistic reinterpretation of *Democracy in America*. By 'equality of conditions' Tocqueville understood the end of ancient societies divided into orders, and not as the reign of individuals always yearning to consume ever more. Further, for him the question of democracy was above all a question of finding the institutional forms equipped to regulate this new configuration. In order to turn Tocqueville into a prophet of democratic despotism and a thinker of consumer society, his two large books must be reduced to the two or three paragraphs of the second book that evoke the risk of a new despotism. Also, one must forget that what Tocqueville dreaded was the possibility that a master-figure, with a centralized State at his disposal, might thereby attain absolute power over depoliticized masses, not the tyranny of democratic opinion that one hears them go on and on about today. The reduction of his account of democracy to a critique of consumer society might have forged a path through some privileged interpretative relays.[14] Above all, however, it is the result of a larger process of effacing the political figure of democracy that has been brought about by means of a well-regulated exchange between sociological description and philosophical judgement.

The stages of this process can be quite easily identified. On the one hand, the 1980s in France witnessed the development of a certain sociological literature – often written, as it so happens, by philosophers – saluting the alliance that had been formed between new forms of consumerism and individual behaviour, between democratic society and its State. All of Gilles Lipovetsky's books and articles capture the supposition quite well. It was a time when pessimistic accounts were arriving from across the Atlantic and beginning to spread throughout France: those of the authors of the Trilateral Commission report, and those of sociologists such as Christopher Lasch and Daniel Bell. The latter called into question the separation between the spheres of the economy, politics and culture. With the development of mass consumption, these spheres were to have become dominated by one supreme value, 'self-realization'. Such hedonism meant breaking with the puritanical traditions that had lent support to both the taking-off of capitalist industry and to achieving political equality. The insatiable appetites emanating from this culture were to have entered into direct conflict with the sacrifices necessitated by the common interest in democratic nations.[15] Now, the accounts by Lipovetsky and others aimed at countering that pessimism. There was no reason, they said, to fear any divergence between forms of mass consumption based on the pursuit of individual pleasure and democratic institutions based on common rule. Quite to the contrary, the very growth of consumer narcissism put individual satisfaction and collective rule in perfect harmony. As a result, individuals were engendered with a much tighter existential commitment to democracy, no longer experienced simply as a matter of constraining institutional forms but as a 'second nature, an environment, an ambiance'. 'The more narcissism grows', Li-povetsky wrote,

> the more legitimacy democracy gains, if only in the mode of cool. Democratic regimes with their party pluralism, their elections, and their freedom of information, are in ever closer affinity with the society of personalized self-service, of try-before-you-buy, and of combinatory freedom . . . It is the very ones who do no more than devote themselves to the private dimension of their life that will remain attached to the democratic functioning of societies by the links woven through the process of persona-lization.[16]

However, rehabilitating 'democratic individualism' against the critiques emanating from America in reality meant performing a double operation. On the one hand, it meant burying an earlier critique of consumer society, namely that undertaken in the 1960s and 1970s when pessimistic and critical accounts of the 'era of opulence' by the likes of J.K. Galbraith or David Riesman were radicalized by Jean Baudrillard in a Marxist mode. The latter denounced the illusions of a 'personalization' entirely subjugated to market imperatives, and it saw in the promises of consumerism the false equality that masked '*absence* of democracy and the non-existence of equality'.[17] The new sociology of narcissistic consumerism eliminated this opposition of represented equality to absent equality. It pointed up the 'process of perso-nalization' that Baudrillard had argued was a lure. In transforming the alienated consumer of the day before into a narcissus who uninhibitedly plays with the objects and the symbols of the market universe, it favourably identified democracy and consumerism. As a result, it complacently offered up this 'rehabilitated' democracy to a more radical critique. To refute the discordance between mass individualism and democratic government meant demonstrating a much more profound evil. It meant positively establishing that democracy was nothing but the reign of the narcissistic consumer varying his or her electoral choices and his or her intimate pleasures alike. To the joyous postmodern sociologists, then, came the response from weighty philosophers *à l'antique*. They reminded us that politics as the Ancients had defined it was an art of living together and a search for the common good; and that what was essential to the very principle of this search and this art was a clear distinction between the domain of common affairs and the egotistical and petty reign of private life and domestic interests. Hence, they said, the 'sociological' portrait of joyous postmodern democracy marked the ruin of politics, henceforth subjugated to a form of society governed by the unique law of consumerist individuality. Against this, it was necessary to restore, with Aristotle, Hannah Arendt and Leo Strauss, a clear sense of a politics freed from the encroachments of democratic consumers. In practice, this consuming individual came quite naturally to be identified with the salaried worker, egotistically defending his or her archaic privileges. Doubtless one will recall the flood of literature that poured out during the strikes and demonstrations in autumn 1995 in France to induce in these privileged individuals an awareness of living together and of the glory of public life that they had just defiled with their egotistical interests.[18] But, more than these circumstantial usages, what counts is the firmly fixed identity between democratic man and individual consumer. The conflict between postmodern sociologists and philosophers *à l'antique* set up this identification all the more easily insofar as the antagonists did no more than present, in a well-regulated duo by a journal ironically entitled *Le Débat*, the two faces of the same coin, the same equation read in two opposing ways.

That was how, in the first part of the operation, democracy was reduced to a state of society. Now we come to the second part of the operation, that is, the one that turns democracy thus defined not simply into a social state that unduly infringes upon the political sphere but into an anthropological catastrophe, a self-destruction of humanity. This further step passed through another well-regulated interplay between philosophy and sociology, one which was less peaceful in its unfolding but yielded the same result. The stage on which this interplay took place was the quarrel over education [*l'École*]. The initial context of the quarrel had to do with educational underachievement, that is to say, the failure of educational institutions to give children from the more modest classes equal chances to the others. So, the quarrel was ultimately over how equality at school or as achieved through the School ought to be understood. The so-called sociological thesis endorsed the works of Bourdieu and Passeron, highlighting the social inequalities that were hidden in apparently neutral forms of the social transmission of knowledge. It proposed that the School be rendered more egalitarian by removing it from the fortress where it had taken up a position sheltered from society: by changing the forms of educational society, and by adapting the educational content to those students most deprived of cultural background. The so-called republican thesis took exactly the opposite tack: bringing School closer to society meant making it more homogeneous to social inequality. So that School could work to achieve equality only to the extent that, within the sheltering walls that separate it from the rest of society, it could devote itself to its proper task: to supply everyone equally, irrespective of origins or social destination, with the universality of knowledge, using for its egalitarian aims the necessarily inegalitarian form of relation obtaining between the one who knows and the one who learns. It was imperative, then, to reaffirm the vocation of School that had been historically embodied in the republican School of Jules Ferry.[19]

The debate therefore seemed to bear on the forms of inequality and the means for achieving equality. The terms of the debate were nonetheless very ambiguous. That the standard-bearing book for this tendency was *De l'École* by Jean-Claude Milner attests to this ambiguity. For what Milner's book said was something quite different to what was allegedly seen in it at the time. It was very little concerned with putting the universal at the service of equality. It was far more concerned with the relations between knowledges, liberties and elites. And, to a far greater extent than Jules Ferry, it followed in Renan's footsteps and his vision of elite experts guaranteeing freedoms in a country threatened by the despotism intrinsic to Catholicism.[20] This opposition between two doctrines, republican and 'sociological', was in fact an opposition between one sociology and another. But the concept of 'republican elitism' was sufficient to mask the ambiguity. The hard kernel of the thesis was concealed under a simple distinction between republican universality and social inequalities and particularities. The debate appeared to be about what public authorities could and should do with the means at their disposal to remedy social inequality. Nonetheless, not long afterwards the perspective was put back on course and the landscape modified. In the stream of allegations about the inexorable rise of people lacking in values owing to the torrent of supermarket values, the root of evil would eventually be identified: it was, to be sure, democratic individualism. The enemy that the republican School confronted, then, was no longer the unequal society from which it sought to rescue pupils, it was the pupil him- or herself, who had become the representative par excellence of democratic humanity – the immature being, the young consumer drunk with equality, and whose charter is the Rights of Man. School, it would soon be said, was badly afflicted by one, and only one, evil, which was embodied in the very beings that had to be taught: equality. And what was undermined along with the authority of the professor was not the universality of knowledges but inequality itself, understood as the manifestation of a 'transcendence':

> No longer having any place for transcendence of any kind, the individual becomes elevated into an absolute value; and if there is anything sacred left it is again the glorification of the individual, by dint of democracy and human rights . . . So that is how the professor's authority has been undermined: with the advance of equality, the teacher has become nothing but an ordinary worker faced with [service] users, and finds himself compelled to discuss things equal to equal with his students, who themselves end up being put in the position of judging their schoolmaster.[21]

The republican schoolmaster, conveyor of the universal knowledge that renders virgin souls equal, simply becomes, then, the representative of an adult humanity in the process of disappearing at the hands of a generalized reign of immaturity; the schoolmaster becomes the last witness of civilization, vainly opposing the 'subtleties' and 'complexities' of his thought to the 'impenetrable wall' of a world doomed to the monstrous reign of adolescence. He becomes the disillusioned spectator of the great catastrophe of civilization, the synonyms of which are consumerism, equality, democracy and immaturity. Before him stands 'the adolescent-punk who, against Kant and Plato, demands the right to his or her own opinion', that is, the representative of the inexorable spiral of democracy drunk with consumption, attesting to the end of culture, if not the becoming culture of everything, to the 'hypermarket of lifestyles' and 'turning the world into a "club-Med"', and to the 'plunging of all of existence into the sphere of consumption'.[22] It is pointless to enter into the details of the endless literature which for some time has, week in week out, warned us about the new manifestations of 'package-deal democracy' and of the 'poison of fraternity':[23] the howlers of schoolchildren avering the devastating effects of the equality of users; the demonstrations of young, illiterate 'alterglobalists' 'drunk with springtime generosity';[24] reality TV programmes offering alarming testimony to the sort of totalitarianism Hitler would not have dreamt of;[25] and a young woman who completely fabricates a racist attack because of a cult of victims that is itself 'inseparable from the development of democratic individualism'.[26] These incessant denunciations of the democratic ruining of all thought and all culture do not only have the advantage of proving a contrario the inestimable heights of the thought, and the unfathomable depth of the culture, of those who loudly announce them – something it would often be much more difficult to do directly. More profoundly, such denunciations permit all these phenomena to be placed on one and the same plane in being related to one and the same cause. The fatal 'democratic' equivalence of everything is indeed first and foremost the product of a method that has only one explanation for every phenomenon, whether it be a social movement, a religious or

ethnic conflict, changing trends, or advertising or other campaigns. This is how the young girl who, in the name of her
father's religion, refuses to remove her headscarf at school, the
schoolchild who opposes the rationality of the Koran to that
of science, and the schoolchild who physically attacks teachers
or Jewish students, will all find their attitudes attributed to the
reign of the democratic individual, unaffiliated and altogether
cut off from transcendence. And the figure of the democratic
consumer drunk on equality will, according to the mood and
the needs of the cause, be identified with the wage earner, with
the unemployed occupying the Unemployment Office, or with
the illegal immigrant detained in airport detention centres.
There is no need to be surprised if the representatives of this
consuming passion that excite the greatest fury in our ideologues are generally those whose capacity to consume is the
most limited. Indeed, the denunciation of 'democratic individualism' works, at little cost, to make coincide two theses: the
classic thesis of property-owners (the poor always want more),
and the thesis of refined elites – there are too many individuals,
too many people claiming the privileges of individuality. This
is how the dominant intellectual discourse meets up with those
censitaire[27] and knowing elites of the nineteenth century:
individuality is a good thing for the elites; it becomes a disaster
for civilization if everybody has access to it.

Such is the way politics in its entirety is accounted for by
an anthropology that knows but one opposition: that between an adult humanity faithful to tradition, which it
institutes as such, and a childish humanity whose dream
of engendering itself anew leads to self-destruction. It is this
change of register that is recorded with a greater conceptual
elegance by *Les Penchants criminels de l'Europe démocratique*.
The theme of 'limitless society' sums up most succinctly

the abundant literature that rolls into a single figure called
'democratic man' the hypermarket consumer, the adolescent
who refuses to take off her headscarf, and the homosexual
couple who want to have children. Above all, it sums up the
double metamorphosis by which democracy has come to be
attributed with engendering both the form of social homogeneity recently accounted for by totalitarianism and the self-
generating growth inherent to the logic of Capital.[28] In such
a way, this theme marks the ultimate achievement of the
French rereading of the democratic double bind. The theory
of the double bind opposed good democratic government to
the double excess of political democratic life and mass
individualism. The French rereading suppresses the tension
of these contraries. Democratic life becomes the apolitical life
of the indifferent consumer of commodities, minority rights,
the culture industry, and children produced in laboratories. It
comes to be identified purely and simply with 'modern
society', which in the same blow is transformed into a
homogeneous anthropological configuration. It is obviously
not irrelevant if today's most radical denouncer of democratic crime was only twenty years ago the flag-bearer for a
secular and republican School. Because it is precisely in
relation to the question of education that the meaning of
some key words – republic, democracy, equality, society –
has radically changed. The question yesterday was about the
equality peculiar to the republican School and its relation to
social inequality. The question today is only about the
process of transmitting knowledge that has to be saved from
the self-destructive tendency being born in democratic society. The issue yesterday concerned transmitting the universality of knowledge and its egalitarian power. What it
comes down to transmitting today, and what the name 'Jew'

typifies for Milner, is simply the principle of birth, the principle of sexual division and of kinship.

Fathers of families who commit their children to 'studying the Pharisees' can then take the role of the republican instructor that wrests children from the familial reproduction of the social order. And good government, as opposed to democratic corruption, no longer need hold on to, by equivocation, the name of democracy. It used to be known by the name 'republic'. But 'republic' is not originally the name of the government of law, of the people, and of its representatives. Since Plato, 'republic' is the name of the government that assures the reproduction of the human herd by protecting it from its bulging appetite for individual goods and collective power. Which is why it can take on another name, a name which traverses, furtively but decisively, this demonstration of democratic crime: good government today rediscovers the name that it had before it had to make way for the name of democracy. That name is pastoral government. Democratic crime has its origin, then, in the primitive scene that consists in forgetting the pastor.[29]

Not long beforehand this had been made explicit in a book entitled *Le Meurtre du pasteur* [The Murder of the Shepherd].[30] This book has one undeniable merit: in illustrating the logic of unities and totalities employed by the author of *Les Penchants criminels de l'Europe démocratique*, it also gives a concrete figure to the 'transcendence' so bizarrely invoked by the new champions of the secular and republican School. The distress of democratic individuals, it says, is that of people who have lost the standard by which the One can be harmonized with the multiple and everyone can unite in a whole. This standard cannot be based on any human convention but only in the care of the divine pastor, who looks after both the whole flock and each member of it. This standard manifests itself in a power that democratic speech will forever lack, the power of the Voice, the shock which all Hebrews felt on that night of fire, whilst the human shepherd, Moses, was given the exclusive responsibility of listening to and of explaining the Word, according to whose teachings he was to organize his people.

Henceforth everything can be simply explained by the evils specific to 'democratic man' and by the basic division of humanity into a humanity that is faithful, and one that is not, to the law of kinship. An attack on the law of kinship is above all an attack on the sheep's bond to its father and divine shepherd. In place of the Voice, the Moderns, Benny Lévy tells us, have put man-god or the people-king, that indeterminate humanity of human rights that the theoretician of democracy, Claude Lefort, had turned into the occupier of an empty place. Instead of 'the Voice toward Moses' we are governed by a 'dead-man-god'. Though it is only capable of governing by making itself into the guarantor of 'petty pleasures', capitalizing on our great distress as orphans condemned to wander in the empire of the void, meaning equally the reign of democracy, of the individual, or of consumption.[31]

2

Politics, or the Lost Shepherd

We are led to understand, then, that the evil lies further in the past. The democratic crime against the order of kinship is above all political crime, that is to say, simply an organization of the human community without any relation to a God-the-father. Under the name democracy, what is being implicated and denounced is politics itself. Now, politics was not born with modern unbelief. Before the Moderns cut off the heads of kings so they could fill up their shopping trolleys at leisure, there were the Ancients, and first of all those Greeks, who severed links with the divine shepherd and set down, under the double name of philosophy and politics, the public record of this farewell. The 'murder of the shepherd', Benny Lévy informs us, is there for all to see in Plato's texts. It is in the *Statesman*, for example, where he evokes the age when the divine shepherd himself directly governed the human flock. And it is in the fourth book of the *Laws*, where he evokes the golden reign of the god Cronus, who knew that no man could govern others without becoming bloated on injustices and excesses, and who resolved the problem by giving the human tribes leaders chosen from the superior race of daimones. But Plato, that reluctant contemporary of the men who claimed that power belonged to the people, not being able to oppose to these men anything except a 'care of the self' incapable of bridging the distance between the many and the whole, effectively countersigned the farewell, relegating the reign of Cronus and the divine shepherd to the era of fables. But he did this at the cost of compensating for the absence of this fable by means of another fable, that of a 'republic' founded on the 'beautiful lie' according to which God, in order to assure a good order in the community, had put gold in the soul of the governors, silver in those of the warriors, and iron in those of the artisans.

Let's grant it to the representative of God: it is quite true that politics is defined in contradistinction to the model of the shepherd feeding his flock. It is just as true that one can object to this separation, by staking a claim, on behalf of the divine shepherd or the human shepherds who interpret his voice, to the government of his people. The price to pay for this is that democracy is effectively only ever the 'empire of nothing', the latest figure of political separation calling for us to turn back, from the pit of despair, toward the forgotten shepherd. If this were the case, the discussion would be rapidly brought to a close. But it is possible to look at things another way, and ask how turning back toward the lost shepherd has come to impose itself as the ultimate consequence of a certain account of democracy conceived as the society of individual consumers. The aim here is not to discover what this politics represses, but inversely to look at what of politics is repressed by this account in which democracy is made out to be a state of excesses and distress from which we can only be saved by some god. So, let's look at the Platonic text from another angle: not from the viewpoint of bidding farewell to the shepherd announced by Plato in the *Statesman*, but on the contrary from the point of view of the nostalgic holding on to the shepherd, of the latter's obstinate presence at the core of the *Republic*, where he serves as the reference point by which an opposition between good government and democratic government is established.

Plato reproaches democracy for two things that at first sight seem opposed, but that on the contrary are strictly articulated to one another. On the one hand, democracy is the rule of abstract law, opposed to the solicitude of the doctor or shepherd. The virtue of the shepherd and the doctor is expressed in two ways: their science is opposed first to the appetite of the petty tyrant, insofar as it is exercised purely for the benefit of those they care for; but it is also opposed to the laws of the democratic city because, in contrast to the latter, this science can be adapted to any particular case – to each particular sheep and each particular patient. The laws of democracy profess, on the contrary, to be applicable in all cases. As such they are like prescriptions that a doctor away on voyage would have left once and for all, regardless of the illness or treatment required. But this universality of the law is a deceptive appearance. In the immutability of the law, it is not the universality of the Idea that democratic man honours, but the instrument of his own good pleasure. In modern terms, it will be said that, underneath the universal citizen of the democratic constitution, we must recognize the real man, that is to say, the egotistical individual of democratic society.

This brings us to the core of the matter. Plato is the first one to invent that mode of sociological reading we declare to be proper to the modern age, the interpretation that locates underneath the appearances of political democracy an inverse reality: the reality of a state of society where it is the private, egotistical man who governs. For him, democratic law, then, is nothing but people's pleasure for its own sake, the expression of the liberty of individuals whose sole law is that of varying mood and pleasure, without any regard for collective order. The term democracy, then, does not simply mean a bad form of government and political life. It strictly means a style of life that is opposed to any well-ordered government of the community. Democracy, Plato tells us in Chapter VIII of the *Republic*, is a political regime that is not one. It does not have a constitution because it has all of them. It is a constitutional bazaar, a harlequin's outfit such as is preferred by men for whom the great issue is the consumption of pleasures and rights. But it is not only the reign of individuals who do anything they please. It is properly the regime that overturns all the relations that structure human society: its governors have the demeanour of the governed and the governed the demeanour of governors; women are the equals of men; fathers accustom themselves to treating their sons as equals; the foreigner and the immigrants are the equals of citizens; the schoolmaster fears and flatters the pupils who, in turn, make fun of him; the young are the equals of the old and the old imitate the young; even the beasts are free and the horses and asses, conscious of their liberty and dignity, knock over anyone who does not yield to them in the street.[32]

Nothing is missing, as you can see, from the census of evils that, at the dawn of the third millennium, the triumph of democratic equality has brought us: reign of the bazaar and its colourful goods, equality between the schoolmaster and the pupil, the resignation of authority, the cult of the young, of children, and of animals. All that the long list of deplorable misdeeds of mass individualism in the age of supermarkets and mobile telephones does is add a few modern accessories to the Platonic fable of the untameable democratic ass.

We might be amused by this, but even more be surprised by it. Are we not continually reminded that we live in the age of technology, of modern States, of sprawling cities and of the global market, an age which no longer has anything to do with those small Greek towns which were once the sites of invention of democracy? The conclusion we are invited to draw from this is that democracy is a political form belonging to another age and unsuitable for ours, at least not without serious modifications and, in particular, not without considerably recanting on the utopia of the power of the people. But if democracy is a thing of the past, then how are we to make sense of the fact that the description of the democratic village elaborated 2500 years ago by an enemy of democracy can be taken as the exact portrait of democratic man at a time of mass consumption and global networks? Greek democracy, so we are told, was appropriate to a form of society that no longer has anything to do with ours. But immediately after this has been posited we are shown that the society to which it was appropriate has exactly the same characteristics as ours. How are we to make sense of this paradoxical relation between a radical difference and a perfect similitude? By way of explanation, I will offer the following hypothesis: the still-applicable portrait of democratic man is the product of an operation, at once inaugural and indefinitely renewed, that aims to ward off an impropriety pertaining to the very principle of politics. The entertaining sociology of a people comprised of carefree consumers, obstructed streets and inverted social roles wards off the presentiment of a more profound evil: that the unnameable democracy is not a form of society refractory to good government and adapted to the lowest common denominator, but the very principle of politics, the principle that institutes politics in founding 'good' government on its own absence of foundation.

To grasp this, let's take up the list of inversions that manifest democratic excess: governors are like the governed, the young like the old, slaves like their masters, pupils like teachers, animals like their masters. Everything here is of course upside down. But this disorder is reassuring. If all the relations are inverted at the same time, then it seems that they are all of the same nature, that all these subversions express the same inversion of the natural order – and hence it appears that this order exists and that the political relation also pertains to that nature. The entertaining portrait of the disorder of both democratic man and society is a way of putting things in order: if democracy inverts the relation of the governing and the governed in the same way it inverts all the other relations, then it confirms a contrario that this relation really is homogeneous to the others, and that governors and governed can be distinguished by means of a principle of distinction that is as certain as the relation between those who beget and those who are begotten, those who come first and those who come after: a principle that assures continuity between the order of society and the order of government, because it firstly assures the continuity between the order of human convention and that of nature.

Let's refer to this principle as *arkhè*. As Hannah Arendt reminded us, in Greek this word means at once commandment and commencement. She logically concluded from this fact that, for the Greeks, it signified the unity of the two. *Arkhè* is the commandment of he who commences, of what comes first.

It is the anticipation of the right to command in the act of commencing and the verifying of the power of commencing in the exercise of commanding. The ideal is thus defined of a government which consists in realizing the principle by which the power of governing commences, of a government which consists in exhibiting *en acte* the legitimacy of its principle. Those who are capable of governing are those who have the dispositions that make them appropriate for the role, those who are capable of being governed are those who have dispositions complementary to the former.

It is here that democracy creates trouble, or rather that it reveals the trouble. This trouble is something that manifests itself in the third book of the *Laws*[33] in a list echoing the list of perturbed natural relations that in the *Republic* presented us with the portrait of democratic man. Given that in every city there are governors and governed, men who exercise the *arkhè* and men who submit to its authority, the Athenian undertakes a census of the titles required to occupy one or other of the positions, in the cities as in the home. These titles are seven in total. Four of them are presented as differences relating to birth: naturally those who are born first or who are highborn command. Such is the power of parents over their children, the old over the young, masters over their slaves, and highborn people over men of no account. Then come two other principles that also express nature if not birth. First, we have 'the law of nature' celebrated by Pindarus, the power of the strongest over the weakest. This title of course is bound to provoke controversy: how to define the strongest? In the *Gorgias* this term is shown to be totally indeterminate and the conclusion is drawn that this power can only be made sense of if identified with the virtue of those who know. Such is precisely the sixth title inventoried: the power which is accomplished by the law of nature properly understood, the authority of those who know over those who are ignorant. Each of these titles fulfils two prerequisites. First, each defines a hierarchy of positions. Secondly, each defines this hierarchy in continuity with nature: continuity by the intermediary of familial and social relations for the first four; direct continuity for the last two. The former titles base the order of the city on the law of kinship. The latter assert that this order has a superior principle: those who govern are not at all those who are born first or highborn, but those who are best. That is effectively when politics commences: when the principle of government is separated from the law of kinship, all the while claiming to be representative of nature; when it invokes a nature that cannot be confounded with the simple relation to the father of the tribe or to the divine father.

That is where politics begins. But that is also where, as it attempts to separate out the excellence specific to it from the sole right of birth, it encounters a strange object, a seventh title to occupy the superior and inferior positions, a title that is not a title, and that, the Athenian tells us, is nevertheless considered to be the most just: the title of that authority that has the 'favour of heaven and fortune': the choice of the god of chance, the drawing of lots, i.e., the democratic procedure by which a people of equals decides the distribution of places.

Therein lies the scandal: the scandal for well-to-do people unable to accept that their birth, their age, or their science has to bow before the law of chance; scandal too for those men of God who would have us all be democrats on the condition that we avow having had to kill a father or a shepherd for it, and hence that we are infinitely guilty, are in inexpiable debt to this father. And yet the 'seventh title' shows us that breaking with the power of kinship does not require any sacrifice or sacrilege.

All it requires is a throw of the dice. The scandal is simply the following: among the titles for governing there is one that breaks the chain, a title that refutes itself: the seventh title is the absence of title. Such is the most profound trouble signified by the word democracy. It's not a question here of a great howling animal, a proud ass, or an individual pursuing pleasure for his or her own sake. Rather is it clearly apparent that these images are ways of concealing the heart of the problem. Democracy is not the whim of children, slaves, or animals. It is the whim of a god, that of chance, which is of such a nature that it is ruined as a principle of legitimacy. Democratic excess does not have anything to do with a supposed consumptive madness. It is simply the dissolving of any standard by which nature could give its law to communitarian artifice via the relations of authority that structure the social body. The scandal lies in the disjoining of entitlements to govern from any analogy to those that order social relations, from any analogy between human convention and the order of nature. It is the scandal of a superiority based on no other title than the very absence of superiority.

Democracy first of all means this: anarchic 'government', one based on nothing other than the absence of every title to govern. But there are many ways of dealing with this paradox. One can simply exclude the democratic title because it is in contradiction with every title to govern. One can also refuse to accept that chance is the principle of democracy, thereby disjoining democracy and the drawing of lots. That is how our moderns have done it, experts, as we saw, at alternately playing on the supposed difference or the similitude of the times. The drawing of lots, so they say, was fitting for ancient times in those small towns with little economic development. How could our modern societies, made of so many delicately interlocking cogs, be governed by individuals chosen by drawing lots, individuals who know nothing of the science of such fragile equilibria? We have found more fitting principles and means for democracy: representation of the sovereign people by elected members; and a symbiosis between the elite, elected representatives of the people, and the elites educated in our schools about the mechanisms by which our societies function.

But differences in time and scale are not the heart of the matter.[34] If the drawing of lots appears to our 'democracies' to be contrary to every serious principle for selecting governors, this is because we have at once forgotten what democracy meant and what type of 'nature' it aimed at countering. If, conversely, the question of the part to assign to the drawing of lots remained active in reflections on democratic and republican institutions from the time of Plato to that of Montesquieu; if aristocratic republicans and thinkers little concerned with equality accepted it, that is because the drawing of lots was the remedy to an evil at once much more serious and much more probable than a government full of incompetents: government comprised of a certain competence, that of individuals skilled at taking power through cunning. The drawing of lots has since been the object of a formidable work of forgetting.[35] We habitually oppose the justice of representation and the competence of governors to arbitrary justice and the mortal risks of incompetence. But the drawing of lots has never favoured the incompetent over the competent. If it has become unthinkable for us today, this is because we are used to regarding as wholly natural an idea that certainly was neither natural for Plato, nor any more natural for French and American constitutionalists two centuries ago: that the first title that calls forward those who merit occupying power is the fact of desiring to exercise it.

Plato knew, though, that chance cannot be so easily pushed aside. Of course, he puts all the desirable irony into recollecting the principle regarded in Athens as that 'favoured by heaven and fortune' and as supremely just. But he retains in this list this title that is not one. And it is not simply because the Athenian is drawing up an inventory that he cannot exclude from the investigation the principle that regulates the organization of his city. There are two more profound reasons for his doing this. The first is that the democratic procedure of drawing lots is compatible with the principle of the power of experts on one point, which is essential: good government is the government of those who do not desire to govern. If there is one category to exclude from the list of those who are capable for governing it is in any case those who set their sights on obtaining power. Besides, we know from the *Gorgias* that, in the eyes of the latter, the philosopher has all the vices he attributes to the democrats. The philosopher, too, embodies the inversion of all natural relations of authority; he is the old man who plays at being a child and teaches the young to despise their fathers and educators; the man who breaks with every tradition that people of substance in the city, and who are for this reason called upon to govern it, pass down from generation to generation. The philosopher-king has at least this point in common with the people-king: some divine chance must make him king without him having desired it.

There is no just government without chance playing a role, that is, without a part for that which contradict any identification of the exercise of government with the exercise of a power both desired and conquered. Such is the paradoxical principle involved whenever the principle of government is disjoined from natural and social differences, in other words, whenever there is politics. And such is the stake of the Platonic discussion about the 'government of the strongest'. How to think politics if it can be neither an extension of differences, that is, of natural and social inequalities, nor a place to be seized by professionals with cunning? But if the philosopher is to pose the question, the condition of his posing it is that democracy must have already – without having had to kill any king or shepherd – proposed the most logical and the most intolerable of responses: the condition under which a government is political is that it is founded on the absence of any title to govern.

This is the second reason why Plato cannot eliminate the drawing of lots from his list. The 'title that is not one' produces a retroactive effect on the others, a doubt concerning the legitimacy they lay claim to. They are, to be sure, real entitlements to govern to the extent that they define a natural hierarchy between governors and governed. But exactly what kind of government they found remains to be seen. That the highborn distinguish themselves from the lowborn is something some people wish would be acknowledged so they can call their government an aristocracy. But Plato knew perfectly well what Aristotle would state in his *Politics*: that those called the 'best' in the life of cities are basically the richest, and that an aristocracy is never anything but an oligarchy, that is, government by wealth. Politics effectively begins whenever the power of birth is undermined, whenever the power of the highborn who lay claim to some founding god of the tribe is declared for what it is: the power of property-owners. And this is well highlighted by the reform Cleisthenes made in instituting Athenian democracy. Cleisthenes recomposed Athens' tribes by artificially combining, via a counter-natural procedure, demes – that is, territorial circumscriptions – that were geographically separated. In so doing, he destroyed the indistinct power of the aristocrat-proprietor-inheritors of the god of place. It is very precisely this dissociation that the word democracy means. The criticism about democracy's 'criminal tendencies' is therefore correct on one point: democracy signifies a rupture with the order of kinship. Only this critique forgets that it is exactly this rupture that realizes, in the most literal manner, exactly what this critique calls for: a structural heterotopy between the principle of government and the principle of society.[36] Democracy is not a modern 'limitlessness' which allegedly destroys the heterotopy necessary to politics. It is on the contrary the founding power of this heterotopy, the primary limitation of the power of forms of authority that govern the social body.

For, supposing that the titles to govern cannot be contested, the problem is to know what government of the community can be deduced from them. The authority of the eldest over the youngest reigns in families, of course, and one can imagine a government of the city modelled on it. One will qualify it accurately in calling it a gerontocracy. The power of the learned over the ignorant prevails with good reason in schools and one could institute, in its image, a power that would be called a technocracy or an epistemocracy. In such a manner, it is possible to establish a list of governments based on the respective titles to govern. But a single government will be missing from the list, precisely political government. If politics means anything it means something that is added to all these governments of paternity, age, wealth, force and science, which prevail in families, tribes, workshops and schools and put themselves forward as models for the construction of larger and more complex human communities. Something additional must come; a power, as Plato put it, that comes from the heavens. But only two sorts of government have ever come from the heavens: the government of mythical times, i.e., the direct reign of the powerful divine shepherd over the human flock or the daimones that Cronus appointed to the leadership of the tribes; and the government of divine chance, the drawing of lots for governors, that is, democracy. The philosopher strives to eliminate democratic disorder in order to found true politics, but he can only do so on the basis of this disorder itself, which severs the link between the leaders of the city tribes and the daimones serving Cronus.

This is exactly the problem. There is a natural order of things according to which assemblies of men are governed by those who possess titles to govern them. In history, we've known two great entitlements to govern: one that is attached to human or divine kinship, that is, the superiority of birth; and another that is attached to the organization of productive and reproductive activities, that is, the power of wealth. Societies are usually governed by a combination of these two powers to which, in varying degrees, force and science lend their support. But if the elders must govern not only the young but the learned and the ignorant as well, if the learned must govern not only the ignorant but also the rich and the poor, if they must compel the obedience of the custodians of power and be understood by the ignorant, something extra is needed, a supplementary title, one common to those who possess all these titles but also to those who do not possess them. Now, the only remaining title is the anarchic title, the title specific to those who have no more title for governing than they have for being governed.

This is what of all things democracy means. Democracy is not a type of constitution, nor a form of society. The power of the people is not that of a people gathered together, of the majority, or of the working class. It is simply the power peculiar to those who have no more entitlements to govern than to submit. One cannot rid oneself of this power in denouncing the tyranny of majorities, the stupidity of the 'great animal', or the frivolity of individualist consumers. For then one must get rid of politics itself. Politics exists only if there is a supplementary title for those who function in the ordinary run of social relations. The scandal of democracy, and of the drawing of lots which is its essence, is to reveal that this title can be nothing but the absence of title, that the government of societies cannot but rest in the last resort on its own contingency. There are people who govern because they are the eldest, the highest-born, the richest, or the most learned. There are models of government and practices of authority based on this or that distribution of places and capabilities. Such is the logic that I've proposed be thought under the name of 'police'.[37] But if the power of elders must be more than a gerontocracy, and the power of the rich more than a plutocracy, if the ignorant are to understand that they have to obey the orders of the learned, their power must rest on a supplementary title, the power of those who have no other property that predisposes them more to governing than to being governed. Their power must become a political power. And a political power signifies in the last instance the power of those who have no natural reason to govern over those who have no natural reason to be governed. The power of the best cannot ultimately be legitimated except via the power of equals.

This is the paradox that Plato encounters in the government of chance and that, in his furious and amusing repudiation of democracy, he must nevertheless take into account when portraying governors as men without properties that only a happy coincidence has called upon to occupy this place. It is

this paradox that Hobbes, Rousseau and all the modern
thinkers of the contract and sovereignty in their turn encounter
through the questions of consent and legitimacy. Equality is
not a fiction. All superiors experience this as the most com-
monplace of realities. There is no master who does not sit back
and risk letting his slave run away, no man who is not capable
of killing another, no force that is imposed without having to
justify itself, and hence without having to recognize the irre-
ducibility of equality needed for inequality to function. From
the moment obedience has to refer to a principle of legitimacy,
from the moment it is necessary for there to be laws that are
enforced qua laws and institutions embodying the common of
the community, commanding must presuppose the equality of
the one who commands and the one who is commanded.
Those who think they are clever and realist can always say
that equality is only the fanciful dream of fools and tender
souls. But unfortunately for them it is a reality that is constantly and everywhere attested to. There is no service that is
carried out, no knowledge that is imparted, no authority that is
established without the master having, however little, to speak
'equal to equal' with the one he commands or instructs.
Inegalitarian society can only function thanks to a multitude
of egalitarian relations. It is this intrication of equality in
inequality that the democratic scandal makes manifest in order
to make it the basis of public power. Only it is not the case, as is
usually said, that the equality of the law exists to correct or
attenuate inequalities in nature. This is because 'nature' itself is
redoubled, because natural inequality can only be carried
through on the presupposition of a natural equality that assists
and contradicts it: impossible otherwise for pupils to understand their schoolmasters or for the ignorant to obey the
government of experts. There will be those who say that the

army and the police force are there for that. But it is still necessary that these latter understand the orders of the experts and the interest they have in obeying them, and so on.

This is what politics requires and what democracy contributes to it. For politics to exist a title of exception is required, a title that is added to those by which societies, large and small, are 'normally' ruled, and which in the last analysis come down to those of birth and wealth. Wealth aims at endless growth, but it does not have the power to transcend itself. Birth asserts its claim to transcendence, but the price of doing so is to leap from human kinship to divine kinship. It founds a government of shepherds, thereby resolving the problem, but at the cost of eliminating politics. What remains is the extraordinary exception, the power of the people, which is not the power of the population or of the majority, but the power of anyone at all, the equality of capabilities to occupy the positions of governors and of the governed. Political government, then, has a foundation. But this foundation is also in fact a contradiction: politics is the foundation of a power to govern in the absence of foundation. State government is only legitimate insofar as it is political. It is political only insofar as it reposes merely on an absence of foundation. This is what democracy means when accurately understood as a 'law of chance'. The customary complaints about democracy's ungovernability in the last instance come down to this: democracy is neither a society to be governed, nor a government of society, it is specifically this ungovernable on which every government must ultimately find out it is based.

3

Democracy, Republic, Representation

The democratic scandal simply consists in revealing this: there will never be, under the name of politics, a single principle of the community, legitimating the acts of governors based on laws inherent to the coming together of human communities. Rousseau was right to denounce the vicious circle that Hobbes gets himself into in claiming to prove the natural unsociability of humans by arguing on the basis of court intrigues and the malicious gossip of salons. But in describing nature on the basis of society, Hobbes did show that it is vain to try to find any origin of the community in some kind of innate virtue of sociability. If the quest for the origin easily mixes up the before and the after, then this is because it always comes after the event. The philosophy that seeks the principles of good government, or the reasons for which humans endow themselves with governments, comes after democracy, which itself comes after, by interrupting the timeless logic according to which societies are governed by those who have a title to exercise their authority over those who are predisposed to submit to it.

The term democracy, then, does not strictly designate either a form of society or a form of government. 'Democratic society' is never anything but an imaginary portrayal designed to support this or that principle of good government. Societies, today as yesterday, are organized by the play of oligarchies. There is, strictly speaking, no such thing as democratic government. Government is always exercised by the minority over the majority. The 'power of the people' is therefore necessarily also heterotopic to inegalitarian society and to oligarchic government. It is what divides government from itself by dividing society from itself. It is therefore also what separates the exercise of government from the representation of society.

People like to simplify the question by returning it to the opposition between direct democracy and representative democracy. One can then simply play on the difference between times, and the opposition between reality and utopia. So, one says that direct democracy was good for Ancient Greek cities or Swiss cantons of the Middle Ages, where the whole population of free men could gather in a single place. But for our vast nations and our modern societies only representative democracy is suitable. The argument is not as probative as it is hoped to be. At the beginning of the nineteenth century, French representatives saw no difficulty in assembling all the electors of the canton in one administrative centre. All that was required was to keep the number of voters low, which was easily done by reserving the right to vote to those who could afford a poll tax of 300 francs. 'Direct elections constitute the only true representative government' Benjamin Constant said at the time.[38] And Hannah Arendt in 1963 could still see the real power of the people in the form of revolutionary councils, where the only effective political elite was constituted, the elite, self-selected on the ground, of those who took pleasure in concerning themselves with public matters.[39]

Otherwise said, representation was never a system invented to compensate for the growth of populations. It is not a form in which democracy has been adapted to modern times and vast spaces. It is, by rights, an oligarchic form, a representation of minorities who are entitled to take charge of public affairs. Historically, it is always first and foremost states, orders, possessions which are represented, whether they are regarded as entitling one to exercise power, or are occasionally given a consultative voice by a sovereign power. Nor is the vote in itself a democratic form by which the people makes its voice heard. It is originally the expression of a consent that a superior power requires and which is not really such unless it is unanimous.[40] The self-evidence which assimilates democracy to a representative form of government resulting from an election is quite recent in history. Originally representation was the exact contrary of democracy. None ignored this at the time of the French and American revolutions. The Founding Fathers and a number of their French emulators saw in it precisely the means for the elite to exercise power *de facto*, and to do so in the name of the people that representation is obliged to recognize but that could not exercise power without ruining the very principle of government.[41] Rousseau's disciples, for their part, only admitted representation by repudiating the meaning of the word, that is, the representation of particular interests. The general will cannot be divided and the deputies only represent the nation in general. 'Representative democracy' might appear today as a pleonasm. But it was initially an oxymoron.

This is not to say that we must oppose the virtues of direct democracy to the mediations and usurpations of representation, or arraign the misleading appearances of formal democracy before the effectivity of real democracy. It is just as false to identify democracy with representation as it is to make the one the refutation of the other. What democracy means is precisely this: the juridico-political forms of State constitutions and laws never rest upon one and the same logic. What is referred to as 'representative democracy' and what it is more accurate to call the parliamentary system, or, following Raymond Aron, the 'pluralist constitutional regime', is a mixed form: a form of State functioning initially founded on the privilege of 'natural' elites and redirected little by little from its function by democratic struggle. The bloody history of struggles for electoral reform in Great Britain is without doubt the best testimony of this, smugly effaced by the idyllic image of an English tradition of 'liberal' democracy. Universal suffrage is not at all a natural consequence of democracy. Democracy has no natural consequences precisely because it is the division of 'nature', the breaking of the link between natural properties and forms of government. Universal suffrage is a mixed form, born of oligarchy, redirected by democratic combats and perpetually reconquered by oligarchy, which puts its candidates, and sometimes its decisions, to the vote of the electoral body, without ever being able to rule out the possibility that the electoral body will behave like a population that draws lots.

Democracy can never be identified with a juridico-political form. This does not mean it is indifferent to such forms. It means that the power of the people is always beneath and beyond these forms. Beneath, because these forms cannot function without referring in the last instance to that power of incompetents who form the basis of and negate the power of the competent, to this equality which is necessary to the very functioning of the inegalitarian machine. Beyond, because the very forms that inscribe this power are constantly reabsorbed, through the play itself of the governmental machine, into the 'natural' logic of titles to govern, which is a logic of indistinction of the public and the private. As soon as the link with nature is severed, as soon as governments are obliged to represent themselves as instances of the common of the community, separated from the sole logic of relations of authority immanent to the reproduction of the social body, there is a public sphere, which is a sphere of encounters and conflicts between the two opposed logics of police and politics, of the natural government of social competences and the government of anyone and everyone. The spontaneous practices of any government tend to shrink this public sphere, making it into its own private affair and, in so doing, relegating the inventions and sites of intervention of non-State actors to the private domain. Democracy, then, far from being the form of life of individuals dedicated to their private pleasure, is a process of struggle against this privatization, the process of enlarging this sphere. Enlarging the public sphere does not entail, as it is claimed in liberal discourse, asking for State encroachments on society. It entails struggling against the distribution of the public and the private that shores up the twofold domination of the oligarchy in the State and in society.

This enlargement has historically signified two things: the recognition, as equals and as political subjects, of those that have been relegated by State law to the private life of inferior beings; and the recognition of the public character of types of spaces and relations that were left to the discretion of the power of wealth. This first involved struggles to include all those that police logic naturally excluded from voting and

eligibility for office, all those who were not entitled to parti-
cipate in public life because they did not belong to 'society' but
merely to domestic and reproductive life, because their work
belonged to a master or a husband: waged workers long
treated as domestics dependent upon their masters and incapable of having an independent will; and women subordinated
to their husbands' will and relegated to the care of family and
domestic life. It also involved struggles against the natural
logic of the electoral system, which turns representation into
the representation of dominant interests and elections into an
apparatus devoted to procuring consent: official candidacies,
electoral fraud, *de facto* monopolies over candidacies. But this
enlargement also includes all the struggles to assert the public
character of spaces, relations and institutions regarded as
private. These struggles, owing to their sites and objects, have
generally been described as social movements: disputes over
salaries and working conditions, and battles over health and
retirement systems. However, this designation is ambiguous.
In fact it presupposes a given distribution of the political and
the social, or of the public and the private, that is in reality a
political contention pertaining to equality and inequality. The
disputes over salaries were above all disputes about depriva-
tizing the wage relation, about proclaiming that it was neither
a relation of master to servant nor a simple contract formed on
case-by-case basis between two private individuals, but a
public matter affecting the collectivity, and, as a result, something that ought to come within the domain of collective
action, public discussion and legislative regulation. The 'right
to work', claimed by workers' movements in the nineteenth
century first signified this: not the demand for assistance from
a 'Welfare State', to which many have sought to assimilate it,
but for the constitution of work as a structure of collective life

wrested from the sole reign of the law of private interest, and the imposition of limits on the naturally limitless process of the increase of wealth.

For, as soon as it emerges from its initial indistinction, domination is exercised through a logic of distribution of spheres that itself has two means of recourse. In the first place, it claims to separate the domain of public matters from the private interests pertaining to society. In this respect, it declares that, even where it is recognized, the equality of 'men' and of 'citizens' only concerns their relation to the constituted juridico-political sphere, and that even where the people is sovereign it is only so through the actions of its representatives and governors. Domination works through the distinction of the public, which belongs to everyone, and the private, where the liberties of all prevail. These liberties each person has are the liberties, that is the domination, of those who possess the immanent powers of society. It is the empire of the law of the accumulation of wealth. In the second place, the public sphere allegedly purified of all private interest is also a privatized, limited, public sphere, one reserved for the play of institutions and the monopoly of those who work them to their advantage. These two spheres are only separated in principle the better to be united under oligarchic law. The American Founding Fathers and the French partisans of the *régime censitaire*[42] indeed saw no harm in identifying the figure of the property-owner with that of the public man [*l'homme publique*] who is capable of elevating himself above the petty interests of economic and social life. The democratic movement, then, is in fact a double movement of transgressing limits: a movement for extending the equality of public man to other domains of life in common, and in particular to all those that govern the limitlessness of capitalist wealth; another movement for reaffirming the belonging of anyone and everyone to that incessantly privatized public sphere.

This is exactly where the much-commented-on duality of man and citizen came into play. This duality has been denounced by critics from Burke to Agamben, via Marx and Hannah Arendt, in the name of a single logic: if two principles are required for politics instead of only one, it must be because of some deceit or vice. One of the two principles must be illusory, if not both. For both Burke and Arendt, the rights of man are either empty or tautological. They are the rights of bare man; but bare man, the man who belongs to no constituted national community, has no rights. The rights of man, then, are the empty rights of those who have no rights. Or they are the rights of men who belong to a national community. They are, then, simply the rights of the citizens of that nation, the rights of those who have rights, and hence a pure tautology. Marx, conversely, saw the rights of citizens as constituting an ideal sphere whose reality consisted in the rights of man, not bare man, but the male property-owner who enforces the law of his interest, the law of wealth, under the mask of the equal rights of all.

Both of these positions intersect at one essential point: the will, inherited from Plato, to reduce man and the citizen to the couple of illusion and reality; the concern that politics should have one and only one principle. What both positions deny is that the one of politics [*l'un de la politique*] exists only through the an-archic supplement signified by the word democracy. We will freely grant to Hannah Arendt that bare humanity does not possess the rights that belong to it, that it is not a political subject. But neither is the citizen of constitutional texts any more of a political subject. The subject of politics can precisely be identified neither with 'humanity' and the gatherings of a population, nor with the identities defined by constitutional texts. They are always defined by an interval between identities, be these identities determined by social relations or juridical categories. The 'citizen' of revolutionary clubs is the one who refutes the constitutional opposition of active citizens (that is to say, those able to afford the poll tax) and passive citizens. The worker (industrial or otherwise) as political subject is the one who separates himself from his assignation to the non-political, private world that these terms imply. Political subjects exist in the interval between different names of subjects. Man and citizen are such names, names of the common, whose extension and comprehension are litigious and which, for this reason, lend themselves to political supplementation, to an exercise that verifies to which subjects these names can be applied, and what power it is that they bear.

This is how the duality of humanity and the citizen was able to serve the construction of political subjects who staged and challenged the twofold logic of domination, i.e., that which separates the public man from the private individual all the better to shore up the same domination in both spheres. In order to prevent this duality from being identified with the opposition between reality and illusion, it must be further divided. Political action, then, opposes to the police logic that separates into spheres another usage of the same juridical text, another staging of the duality between public man and private individual. It overturns the distribution of terms and places by playing man against citizen and citizen against man. As a political name, the citizen opposes the rule of equality fixed in law and in principle to the inequalities that characterize 'men', that is to say, private individuals subjected to the powers of birth and wealth. And, conversely, the reference to 'man' opposes the equal capacity of everyone to all privatizations of citizenship: those which exclude such and such a part of the population from citizenship, or those which exclude such and such a domain of collective life from the rule of citizen equality. Each of these terms, then, polemically plays the role of the universal that is opposed to the particular. And the opposition of 'bare life' to political existence itself can also be politicized.

This is what was shown by the celebrated syllogism introduced by Olympe de Gouges in Article 10 of her *Declaration of the Rights of Women and the Citizen*: 'Woman has the right to mount the scaffold; she must equally have the right to mount the rostrum.' This reasoning is curiously inserted in the middle of a statement about women's right to freedom of expression, modelled on that of men ('No one shall be disquieted on account of his opinions . . . provided their manifestation does not disturb the public order established by law.') But this curiosity itself marks the torsion of the relation between life and citizenship which establishes the claim that women belong to the sphere of political expression. Women were excluded from the benefits of having citizens' rights in the name of a division between the public and the private spheres. In belonging to the domestic sphere, hence to the world of particularity, they were foreign to the universality of the citizen sphere. De Gouges turns the argument around, basing her position on the argument that makes punishment the 'right' of the guilty party: if women have 'the right to mount the scaffold', if a revolutionary power can condemn them to it, this is because their bare life itself is political. The equality of the death sentence revokes the self-evidence of the distinction of domestic life and political life. Women can therefore claim rights as women and as citizens, an identical right that, however, can only be asserted in the form of the supplement.

In so doing, they refuted with this fact the demonstration made by Burke and Arendt. As both the latter put it: either the rights of man are the rights of the citizen, that is to say, the rights of those who have rights, which is a tautology; or the rights of the citizen are the rights of man. But as bare humanity has no rights, then they are the rights of those who have no rights, which is an absurdity. And yet, caught in the pincers of this alleged logical bind, Olympe de Gouges and her companions manage to insert a third possibility: 'women's and citizen's rights' are the rights of those who have not the rights that they have and have the rights that they have not. They are arbitrarily deprived of the rights that the Declaration attributes to the members of the French nation and the human species without discrimination. But they also exercise, by their action, the citizen's rights that the law refuses them. They demonstrate in this way that they do have the rights denied them. 'Have' and 'not to have' are terms that split into two. And politics is the operation of this splitting into two. The young black woman of Montgomery, Alabama, who, one day in December 1955, decided to remain in her seat on the bus, which was not hers, in this way decided that she had, as a citizen of the United States, the rights she did not have as an inhabitant of a State that banned the use of such seats to individuals with one-sixteenth or more parts of 'non-Caucasian' blood.[43] And the Blacks of Montgomery who, a propos of this conflict between a private person and a transportation company, decided to boycott the company, really acted politically, staging the double relation of exclusion and inclusion inscribed in the duality of the human being and the citizen.

This is what the democratic process implies: the action of subjects who, by working the interval between identities, reconfigure the distributions of the public and the private, the universal and the particular. Democracy can never be identified with the simple domination of the universal over the particular. For the universal is incessantly privatized by police logic, incessantly reduced to a power-share between birth, wealth and 'competence', which is at work in the State as well as in society. This privatization is gladly carried out in the name of the purity of public life, as opposed to the particularities of private life or of the social realm. But this alleged purity is only the purity of a distribution of terms, of a given state of relations between the social forms of the power of wealth and the forms of State privatization of the power of everyone. The argument only bears out what it presupposes: the separation between those who are and are not 'destined' to take charge of public life and the distribution of the public and the private. The democratic process must therefore constantly bring the universal into play in a polemical form. The democratic process is the process of a perpetual bringing into play, of invention of forms of subjectivation, and of cases of verification that counteract the perpetual privatization of public life. Democracy really means, in this sense, the impurity of politics, the challenging of governments' claims to embody the sole principle of public life and in so doing be able to circumscribe the understanding and extension of public life. If there is a 'limitlessness' specific to democracy, then that's exactly where it lies: not in the exponential multiplication of needs or of desires emanating from individuals, but in the movement that ceaselessly displaces the limits of the public and the private, of the political and the social.

It is this displacement inherent to politics itself that so-called republican ideology refuses to accept. This ideology asserts a strict delimitation of spheres between the political and the social and regards the republic as identical to the rule of law, equally applied to all particularities. This is how, in the 1980s, it argued its case for School reform. It propagated the simple doctrine of a secular and republican School that is supposed to impart the same knowledge to everybody irrespective of social differences. It insisted, as a matter of republican dogma, on the separation between instruction, that is, the imparting of knowledge, which is a public matter, and education, which is a private matter. It then ascribed the cause of this 'crisis of the School' to society's having invaded the educational institution, and accused sociologists of being the instruments of that invasion by proposing reforms that consecrated the confusion between education and instruction. Thus understood, the republic appeared to present itself as the rule of equality embodied in the neutrality of the State institution, indifferent to social differences. So, it might be cause for surprise that the principal theoretician of that secular and Republican school today presents as the sole obstacle to the suicide of democratic humanity the law of kinship embodied in the father who urges his children to study the sacred texts of one religion. But the apparent paradox shows precisely the ambiguity concealed by the simple reference to a republican tradition that maintains a separation between State and society.

For the word 'republic' cannot merely signify the equal rule of law for all. 'Republic' is an equivocal term, wrought by the tension implied in the wish to include the excess of politics in the instituted forms of the political. Including this excess means two contradictory things: to entitle it by fixing it in the texts and the forms of community institutions, but also to eliminate it by identifying the laws of the State with the moral values of a society. On the one hand, the modern republic is identified with the reign of a law emanating from a popular will which includes the excess of the demos. But, on the other, including this excess requires a regulating principle: the republic must have not only laws but republican morals too. The republic, then, is a regime of homogeneity between State institutions and societal mores. In this sense, the republican tradition goes back neither to Rousseau nor to Machiavelli. It strictly goes back to the Platonic *politeia*. For the latter is not the reign of equality through the law, of 'arithmetic' equality between equivalent units. It is the reign of geometrical equality, which places those who count for more above those who count for less. Its principle is not the written law that applies equally to everyone, but the education that endows each person and each class with the virtues specific to its place and its function. The republic so understood does not oppose its unity to sociological diversity. For sociology is precisely not a chronicle of social diversity. On the contrary, it is the vision of a homogeneous social body, opposing its internal vital principle to the abstraction of the law. Republicanism and sociology are, in this sense, two names for the same project: to restore beyond the democratic rupture a political order that is homogeneous to the mode of life of a society. This is really what Plato proposes: a community whose laws are not dead formulae but the very respiration of society – the advice of the wise and the movement that the bodies of citizens internalize from birth, expressed through the dancing choruses of the city. This is what sociological science suggested be undertaken in the aftermath of the French Revolution: remedy the 'Protestant', individualist tearing of the ancient social fabric, which was organized on the basis of the privilege of birth; oppose to democratic dispersion the reconstitution of a social body that is evenly distributed in its functions and natural hierarchies, and united by common beliefs.

The republican conception therefore cannot be defined as a limiting of society by the State. It always implies the work of education that establishes or re-establishes harmony through laws and mores, through the system of institutional forms and the disposition of the social body. There are two ways of thinking this education. Some people see it already at work in the social body from which it is simply necessary to extract it: the logics of birth and wealth produce elites with 'capabilities' who have the time and means to enlighten themselves and impose republican standards on democratic anarchy. Such was the thinking of the American Founding Fathers. For others, the system of capabilities has itself been undone and science is required to reconstitute the harmony between State and society. Such was the thinking that founded the educative enterprise of the Third French Republic. But never was this enterprise reducible to the simple model that has been drawn up by the 'republicans' of our time. For its combat was a combat on two fronts. It strove to wrest the elites and the people from the power of the Catholic Church and the monarchy it served. Yet this programme in no way coincided with the project of a separation between society and State, instruction and education. For the nascent republic in effect subscribed to the sociological programme of recreating a homogeneous social fabric to succeed, beyond the democratic and revolutionary rupture, the ancient fabric of monarchy and religion. This is why intertwining instruction and education was essential to it. The sentences that introduce primary school children to the world of reading and writing must be inseparable from the moral virtues that fix their usage. And, at the other end of the chain, one counts on the examples given by Latinate literature, rid of vain philological subtleties, so it can impart its virtues to a ruling elite.

This is also why the republican School is from the start divided between two opposed visions. The programme of Jules Ferry is based on a postulated equation between the unity of science and the unity of the popular will. By identifying republic and democracy as an indivisible social and political order, Ferry called, in the name of Condorcet and the Revolution, for a teaching that would be homogeneous from the highest to the lowest level. Also, his desire to eliminate the barriers between primary, secondary and tertiary, his stand for a school open to the exterior, where primary instruction is based on entertaining 'lessons about things' [*leçons des choses*] rather than on the austere rules of grammar, and for a modern schooling that opens up the same opportunities as classic schooling, will all sound quite bad to the ears of many of our 'republicans'.[44] At any rate, at the time, these proposals elicited the hostility of those who saw in them the invasion of the republic by democracy. Such people campaigned for teaching methods that clearly separated the two functions of the public school: instructing the people about what is useful; and forming an elite capable of elevating itself above the utilitarianism to which the men of the people are destined.[45] For them, the distribution of knowledge always had at one and the same time to involve immersion in a 'milieu' and in a 'body' gearing the people to their social destination. The absolute evil is the confusion of milieus. Now, the root of that confusion regarded as a vice had two equivalent names, egalitarianism and individualism. On this account, 'false democracy', that is 'individualist democracy', leads civilization to the avalanche of evils described by Alfred Fouillée in 1910, and in which the newspaper reader of 2006 will without any trouble recognize the catastrophic effects of May 1968 – sexual liberation and the reign of mass consumerism:

Absolute individualism, whose principles are often adopted by socialists, has it that sons . . . need in no way be united with their families: it approves of them being like any individual X . . . fallen from the sky, able to do anything, having no other rules than the fortunes of their tastes. Everything that can bind men together is like a servile chain to individualist democracy.

It begins to revolt even against the difference between the sexes and against the obligations that difference entails: why raise women differently to men, or separately, for different professions? Put them all together in the same system, and in the same scientific, historical and geographical broth, in the same exercises and make the same careers available to them equally . . . The anonymous individual, asexual, without ancestors, without traditions, without milieu, without bonds of any sort, this – as Taine had foreseen – is the man of false democracy, the one who votes and whose voice counts as one, whether he be called Thiers, Gambetta, Taine, Pasteur, or whether he be called Vacher. The individual will end up alone with his ego, instead of with all the 'collective spirits', instead of all those professional milieus which have, throughout the ages, created bonds of solidarity and maintained traditions of common honour. That will be a triumph for the atomistic individual, that is, for force, number and cunning.[46]

How the atomization of individuals can come to signify the triumph of number and force might remain obscure to the reader. But such is precisely the great subterfuge effected by recourse to the concept of 'individualism'. That individualism is so out of favour with people who otherwise declare their profound disgust for collectivism and totalitarianism is an easily solved enigma. It is not the collectivity in general that is being defended by the denouncer of 'democratic individualism'. It is a certain collectivity, the well-ordered collectivity of bodies, milieus and 'atmospheres' that adapts knowledges to rank under the wise direction of an elite. And it is not individualism as such that is being rejected but the idea that anyone at all can share in its prerogatives. The denunciation of 'democratic individualism' is simply the hatred of equality by which a dominant intelligentsia lets it be known that it is the elite entitled to rule over the blind herd.

It would be unjust to confound the republic of Jules Ferry with that of Alfred Fouillée. On the other hand, it is fair to say that the 'republicans' of our age are much closer to the second than to the first. Much more than inheritors of the Enlightenment tradition and the great dream of a scholarly and equal education of the people, they are inheritors of the great obsession with 'disaffiliation', with 'disunion' [*déliaison*], and with the disastrous mixing of conditions and sexes brought about by the collapse of traditional orders and bodies. It imports above all to understand the tension that inhabits the idea of the republic. The idea of the republic is one of a system of institutions, laws and moral values that eliminate democratic excess by making State and society homogeneous. The School, by means of which the State distributes the elements to educate simultaneously both men and citizens, quite naturally suggests itself as the best institution for realizing that idea. But there are no particular reasons why the distribution of knowledges – mathematics or Latin, philosophy or natural sciences – ought to educate citizens for the republic and not advisors to the prince or clerics in the service of God. The distribution of knowledges is only socially efficacious to the extent that it is also a (re)distribution of positions. To gauge the relation between the two distributions, one must therefore have an additional science. Ever since Plato this royal science has had a name. That name is political science. As it has been dreamt of from Plato to Jules Ferry, political science is what has to unify knowledges and, on the basis of that unity, define a common will and a common leadership for the State and for society. But this science will always be missing the very thing that is necessary for settling the excess constitutive of politics: the determination of the just proportion between inequality and equality. There are, to be sure, all kinds of institutional arrangements that enable States and governments to present oligarchs and democrats with the face that each of them want to see. In the fourth book of his *Politics*, Aristotle created the as yet unsurpassed theory of that art. But there is no science of the just measure between equality and inequality. And there is less of it than ever when conflict erupts between the limitlessness of capitalist wealth and the limitlessness of democratic politics. The republic aims at being the government of democratic equality by dint of a science of the just proportion. But when a god is lacking to provide souls with the right proportion of gold, silver or iron, that science is also lacking. The government of science will always end up a government of 'natural elites', in which the social power of those with expert competences is combined with the power of wealth, at the cost once more of provoking a democratic disorder that displaces the boundaries of the political.

To erase the tension inherent to the republican project to produce homogeneity between State and society means that neo-republican ideology in fact erases politics itself. Its defence of public instruction and political purity, then, comes down to placing politics uniquely in the State sphere, even if it means asking the managers of the State to follow the advice of the enlightened elite. The grandiose republican proclamations of the return to politics in the 1990s have essentially served to support governmental decisions, even when they signalled effacing the political under the exigencies of the limitlessness of global Capital, and to stigmatize as 'populist' backwardness any political struggle against that effacement. The only task outstanding was to attribute, ingenuously or cynically, the limitlessness of wealth to the voracious appetites of democratic individuals, and to make this voracious democracy the major catastrophe by which humanity shall destroy itself.

4

The Rationality of a Hatred

We can now return to the initial terms of our problem: we live in societies and States known as 'democracies', a term by which they are distinguished from societies governed by States without law or with religious law. How are we to understand that, at the heart of these 'democracies', a dominant intelligentsia, whose situation is not obviously desperate and who hardly aspire to live under different laws, day in day out blame all of humanity's misfortunes on a single evil they call democracy?

Let's take things in order. What is meant when it is said that we live in democracies? Strictly speaking, democracy is not a form of State. It is always beneath and beyond these forms. Beneath, insofar as it is the necessarily egalitarian, and necessarily forgotten, foundation of the oligarchic state. Beyond, insofar as it is the public activity that counteracts the tendency of every State to monopolize and depoliticize the public sphere. Every State is oligarchic. One of the theoreticians of the opposition between democracy and totalitarianism quite happily acknowledges it: '*It is impossible to conceive of a regime which in one sense is not oligarchic.*'[47] But oligarchy can give democracy more or less room; it is encroached upon by democratic activity to a greater or lesser extent. In this precise sense, the constitutional forms and practices of oligarchic governments can be said to be more or less democratic. Usually the mere existence of a representative system is regarded as the crucial criterion for defining democracy. But this system itself is an unstable compromise, the result of opposing forces. It tends toward democracy only to the extent that it moves nearer to the power of anyone and everyone. With this in mind, we can specify the rules that lay down the minimal conditions under which a representative system can be declared democratic: short and non-renewable electoral mandates that cannot be held concurrently; a monopoly of people's representatives over the formulation of laws; a ban on State functionaries becoming the representatives of the people; a bare minimum of campaigns and campaign costs; and the monitoring of possible interference by economic powers in the electoral process. Such rules have nothing extravagant about them and in the past many thinkers and legislators, hardly moved by a rash love of the people, have carefully considered them as potential means to maintain a balance of powers, to dissociate the representation of the general will from that of particular interests, and to avoid what they considered as the worst of governments: the governments of those who love power and are skilled at seizing it. All one has to do today to provoke hilarity is list them. With good reason – for what we call democracy is a statist and governmental functioning that is exactly the contrary: eternally elected members holding concurrent or alternating municipal, regional, legislative and/or

ministerial functions and whose essential link to the people is
that of the representation of regional interests; governments
which make laws themselves; representatives of the people that
largely come from one administrative school;[48] ministers or
their collaborators who are also given posts in public or semi-
public companies; fraudulent financing of parties through
public works contracts; businesspeople who invest colossal
sums in trying to win electoral mandates; owners of private
media empires that use their public functions to monopolize
the empire of the public media. In a word: the monopolizing of
la chose publique by a solid alliance of State oligarchy and
economic oligarchy. We see why those who despise 'democratic individualism' do not reproach this system of predation
of the public interest and public goods for anything. In fact,
these forms of over-consumption of public functions do not
come within the province of democracy. The evils of which our
'democracies' suffer are primarily evils related to the insatiable
appetite of oligarchs.

We do not live in democracies. Neither, as certain authors
assert – because they think we are all subjected to a biopo-
litical government law of exception – do we live in camps.
We live in States of oligarchic law, in other words, in States
where the power of the oligarchy is limited by a dual
recognition of popular sovereignty and individual liberties.
We know the advantages of these sorts of States as well as
their limitations. They hold free elections. These elections
essentially ensure that the same dominant personnel is
reproduced, albeit under interchangeable labels, but the
ballot boxes are generally not rigged and one can verify it
without risking one's life. The administration is not corrupt,
except in matters of public contracts where administration is
confounded with the interests of the dominant parties.

Individual liberties are respected, although there are notable exceptions here to do with whatever relates to the protection of borders and territorial security. There is freedom of the press: whoever wants to start up a newspaper or a television station without the assistance of the financial powers will experience serious difficulties, but he or she will not be thrown into prison. The rights of association, assembly and demonstration permit the organization of democratic life, that is, a life which is independent of the State sphere. 'Permit' is obviously an ambiguous word. These freedoms were not the gifts of oligarchs. They were won through democratic action and are only ever guaranteed through such action. The 'rights of man and of the citizen' are the rights of those who make them a reality.

The optimistically minded among us will deduce from this that the oligarchic State of law has brought into being that felicitous balance of contraries by which, according to Aristotle, bad governments approach impossible good government. To all intents and purposes, then, a 'democracy' would be something like an 'oligarchy' that leaves enough room for democracy to feed its passion. The more despondent among us will reverse the argument. Peaceful oligarchic government redirects democratic passions toward private pleasures and renders people insensitive to the public sphere. Just look, they say, at what is happening in France. We have a constitution that has been admirably made so that our country can be well-governed and willingly so: the system known as majoritarianism eliminates parties of the extreme right and gives 'government parties' the means to govern in alternation; it thereby enables the majority, that is, the strongest minority, to govern without opposition for a period of five years and, with an assurance of stability, to take all the measures for ensuring the common good that the unforeseeability of circumstances and long-term forecasts necessitate. On the one hand, that alternation satisfies the democratic taste for change. On the other, as the members of the government parties have done their studies in the same schools as those who are expert in managing the public interest, they tend to adopt the same solutions, giving precedence to the science of experts over the passions of the multitude. A culture of consensus is accordingly created that repudiates the old conflicts, accustoms us to dispassionately objectivizing both the short- and long-term problems that societies encounter, to asking experts for solutions, and to discussing them with representatives qualified in grand social interests. Alas! All these good things have their downside: the multitude, freed of the worry of governing, is left to its private and egotistical passions. Either the individuals composing it are uninterested in public matters and abstain from elections; or they approach them uniquely from the point of view of their interests and consumer whims. In the name of their immediate corporatist interests, they go on strike and hold demonstrations against measures that aim to ensure that their retirement schemes have a future; according to their individual whims they choose whoever pleases them at election time as if they were choosing between the many kinds of bread offered them in trendy bakeries. The result is that the 'protest candidates' total more votes in the elections than the 'government candidates'.

There are many things that we might object to in this argument. Such inevitable criticisms of 'democratic individualism', here as everywhere, are contradicted by the facts. It is not true that we are observing an irresistible rise in the rate of abstention. We have rather had the opportunity to see an admirable civic constancy in the elevated number of voters who persist in mobilizing themselves to choose between identical representatives of a State oligarchy that constantly flaunts its mediocrity, if not its corruption. And the democratic passion that so belittles the 'government candidates' is no consumer whim; it is simply the wish that politics be more than a choice between interchangeable oligarchs. But the argument is best tackled at its strongest point. What it tells us is at once simple and accurate: the admirable system that gives the strongest minority the power to govern without trouble, and to create a majority and an opposition that are in agreement on which policies to implement, leads the oligarchic machine itself to a state of paralysis. What produces this paralysis is the contradiction between two principles of legitimacy. On the one hand, our States of oligarchic law refer to a principle of popular sovereignty. This notion, to be sure, is ambiguous both in principle and in practice. Popular sovereignty is a way of including democratic excess, of transforming into an *arkhè* the anarchic principle of political singularity – the government of those who are not entitled to govern. It has its application in the contradictory system of representation. But the contradiction has never killed the thing that has the tension of contraries as its very principle. The fiction of the 'sovereign people' has therefore served as well as not as a linkage between governmental logic and political practices, which are always practices of dividing the people, of constituting a people that supplements the one that is inscribed in constitutions, represented by parliamentarians, and embodied in the State. The very vitality of our parliaments was until quite recently fuelled and supported by extraparliamentary and even antiparliamentary political action that made politics into a domain of contradictory possibilities, possibilities referring not only to differing opinions but also to opposite worlds.

It is this conflictual equilibrium that has been undermined today. The long decline and brutal collapse of the Soviet system, as well as the weakening of social struggles and movements of emancipation, have allowed a consensual vision to establish itself on the back of an oligarchic system. According to this vision, our basic reality does not leave us the choice to interpret it and merely requires responses adapted to the circumstances, responses which are generally the same, whatever our opinions and aspirations. This reality is called the economy; in other words, the unlimited power of wealth. We saw the difficulty this limitlessness produces for the principle of government. But if it were known how to divide the problem into two, it could be resolved and this solution could give the oligarchic government the royal science that up until now it had only vainly dreamt of. For, indeed, if the limitless movement of wealth is posited as the incontrovertible reality of our world and its future, then it is left to governments, concerned with realistically managing the present and boldly forecasting the future, to take off the clamps that existing inertias within our national States put on its uninhibited development. But inversely, as this deployment is limitless, as it does not bother itself with the specific lot of such and such a population or part thereof on the territory of such and such a State, it falls to governments to bring this uncontrollable and ubiquitous power of wealth under the control of the interests of its populations.

Eliminating national limits for the limitless expansion of capital; bringing the limitless expansion of capital within the limits of the nation: at the intersection of these two tasks the finally discovered figure of the royal science takes shape. It will always be impossible to find the just measure of equality and inequality; impossible, on this basis, to avoid democratic

supplementation, namely, the dividing of the people. Governments and experts, on the other hand, consider it possible to
find the right balance between the limited and the limitless.
This goes by the name of modernization. Modernization is not
the simple task of gearing governments to the harsh realities of
the world. It also implies marrying the principle of wealth and
the principle of science in order to give oligarchy a renewed
legitimacy. At least in the short space of time that the battle for
acquiring and preserving power leaves them, our governments
make managing the local effects of global necessity on populations their essential task. This means that the population under
consideration for management must comprise a single, objec-
tivizable totality in opposition to the people of divisions and
metamorphoses. The principle of the popular vote from then
on becomes problematic. No doubt it imports very little to
consensual logic if the popular decision designates an oligarch
from the right or if it designates one from the left. But there is a
risk in leaving the solutions that depend upon the exclusive
science of experts up to this decision. Our governments'
authority thus gets caught in two opposed systems of legitimation: on the one hand, it is legitimated by virtue of the
popular vote; on the other, it is legitimated by its ability to
choose the best solutions for societal problems. And yet, the
best solutions can be identified by the fact that they do not
have to be chosen because they result from objective knowledge of things, which is a matter for expert knowledge and not
for popular choice.

There was a time when the division of the people was active
enough and science modest enough for the opposing principles
to maintain a coexistence. Today an oligarchic alliance of
wealth and science stakes a claim to all the power and pro-
scribes the possibility that the people divide and multiply. But

the division between principles that is driven away returns from all directions. It returns with the rise of parties of the extreme right, and with identitarian and religious fundamentalist movements which, against the oligarchic consensus, appeal to the old principles of birth and kinship, to a community rooted in the soil, blood and the religion of their ancestors. It returns too in the multiplicity of struggles that reject the global economic necessity that the consensual order turns to good account in order to undermine health systems, retirement schemes and the right to work. It returns lastly within the very functioning of the electoral system when the sole solutions that are imposed on governors and the governed alike are left to the unpredictable decision of the latter. The recent European referendum produced the proof. Those who submitted the question to a referendum were of the mind that this was a vote in the original Western meaning of 'election': a means of getting the people assembled to consent to those who are qualified to guide them. All the more so as the elite experts unanimously asserted that the question was not a question, that the matter was basically about pursuing a logic of accords that is already in existence and in conformity with everybody's interests. The principal surprise of the referendum was this: a majority of voters, conversely, judged that the question was a real question, not a matter for calling for the simple adherence of the population but one for the sovereignty of the people, and so a matter to which this latter could respond no as well as yes. We know the rest.[49] We also know that the oligarchs, their experts and ideologues managed to find the explanation for this misfortune, in fact the same one they find for every disruption to the consensus: if science did not impress its legitimacy upon the people, it is because the people is ignorant. If progress does not progress, it is because of the backward.

One word that all the clerics incessantly chanted captures this explanation: 'populism'. The hope is that under this name they will be able to lump together every form of dissent in relation to the prevailing consensus, whether it involves democratic affirmation or religious and racial fanaticism. And it is hoped that a single principle will come to be ascribed to this thus-constituted ensemble: the ignorance of the backward, the attachment to the past, be it the past of social advantages, of revolutionary ideals, or of the religion of ancestors. Populism is the convenient name under which is dissimulated the exacerbated contradiction between popular legitimacy and expert legitimacy, that is, the difficulty the government of science has in adapting itself to manifestations of democracy and even to the mixed form of representative system. This name at once masks and reveals the intense wish of the oligarch: to govern without people, in other words, without any dividing of the people; to govern without politics. And it enables the expert government to rid itself of the old aporia: how can science govern those who do not understand it? This eternal question encounters a more contemporary one: how exactly to determine this measure, whose secret expert government claims to know, between the good that is procured by the limitlessness of wealth and that which procures its limitation? That is to say, how exactly is the combination of the two desires to liquidate politics effected in royal science – the one that inheres in the exigencies of capitalist limitlessness; and the one that inheres in the oligarchic management of nation-States?

For, in the diversity of their motivations and the incertitude of their formulations, the critique of 'globalization', the resistance to adapting our systems of protection and social security to its constraints, and the rejection of supra-State institutions meet at the same sensitive point: what exactly is the necessity in the name of which these transformations are being carried out? That capital growth and investor interests have laws involving complicated mathematical equations is freely granted. That these laws enter into contradiction with the limits posed by national systems of social legislation is just as obvious. But that these laws are ineluctable historical laws that it is vain to oppose, and that they promise a prosperity for future generations that justifies sacrificing these systems of protection, is no longer a matter of science but of faith. The most intransigent devotees of pure laisser-faire economics often have difficulties demonstrating how the conservation of natural resources can be harmoniously arranged through the play of free competition. And if, using statistical comparisons, it is possible to establish that certain forms of flexibility concerning the right to work create more jobs than they suppress in the medium term, it is more difficult to demonstrate that the free circulation of capital demanding an ever more rapid profitability is a providential law that shall lead humanity to a better future. Faith is required. The 'ignorance' that people are being reproached for is simply its lack of faith. In fact, historical faith has changed camps. Today's faith seems to be the prerogative of governors and their experts. This is because it lends a hand to their deeper compulsion, the natural compulsion for oligarchic government: the compulsion to get rid of the people and of politics. Proclaiming themselves to be simply administrating the local consequences of global historical necessity, our governments take great care to banish the democratic supplement. Through the invention of supra-State institutions which are not States, which are not accountable to any people, they realize the immanent ends of their very practice: depoliticize political matters, reserve them for places that are non-places, places that do not leave any space for the democratic invention of polemic. So the State and their experts can quietly agree amongst themselves. The 'European Constitution' be-fallen by its well-known misfortunes illustrates the logic well. One of the parties in favour of adopting it thought it had found the right slogan: 'Liberalism', it gloated, 'has no need of constitutions.' Unfortunately for it, it was telling the truth: 'liberalism', that is to say – to call things by their name – capitalism, does not make any such claim.[50] In order to func-tion, it has no need that any constitutional order be declared for 'deregulated competition', that is, the free and limitless circula-tion of capital. It requires only that the latter be permitted to function. The mystical honeymoon between capital and the common good are needless for capital. It serves only the ends pursued by oligarchs of State: the constitution of interstate spaces liberated from the need for popular and national legiti-macy.

Ineluctable historical necessity is comprised of nothing except the conjunction of two specific necessities; the limitless growth of wealth; and the growth of oligarchic power. The alleged weakening of nation-States on the European and world scene is a perspective *en trompe l'oeil*. The new division of powers between international capitalism and nation-States tends more toward reinforcing States than toward weakening them.[51] The same States that surrender their privileges to the exigencies of freely circulating capital rediscover them straight away in order to close their borders to the freely circulating poor of the planet in search of work. The war declared on the 'Welfare State' bears witness to the same ambivalence. It is conveniently presented as the end of a situation of assistance and the return to individual responsibilities and the initiatives of civil society. One feigns to hold as abusive gifts from a paternal and tentacular State the institutions of solidarity and security born in worker and democratic struggles and managed or co-managed by the representatives of contributors. Yet in struggling against this mythical State, it is precisely non-State institutions of solidarity that are attacked, institutions that were also sites where different capacities were formed and exercised, capacities for taking care of the common and the common future that were different to those of the government elites. The result of this is the reinforcement of a State that becomes directly responsible for the health and life of individuals. The same State that enters into battle against the institutions of the Welfare State is mobilized to have the feeding tube of a woman in a permanent state of vegetation reconnected. The elimination of the so-called Welfare State is not the withdrawal of the State. It is a redistribution, between a capitalist logic of insurance and direct state-management, of the institutions and functions that intervened between the two. The simplistic opposition between state assistance and individual initiative serves as a mask of the two political stakes of this process and of the conflicts to which it gives rise: the existence of forms of organization of the material life of society that escape the logic of profit; and the existence of places for discussing collective interests that escape the monopoly of the expert government. We know just how much these points were at issue during the French strikes of autumn 1995. Beyond the particular interests of the corporations that had gone on strike, and beyond the government's budgetary calculations, it transpired that the 'social' movement was a democratic movement because it revolved around the fundamental political question: that of the competence of the 'incompetent', of the capacity of anybody at all to judge the relations between individuals and the collectivity, present and future.

This is why the campaign opposing common interest to the retrograde egoism of corporations misfired, as did the 'republican' litany on the distinction between the political and the social. A political movement is always a movement that blurs both the given distribution of the individual and the collective, and the accepted boundary of the political and the social. The oligarchy and its experts have never ceased to experience this in their undertaking to fix the distribution of places and competences. But what puts the oligarchy in a quandary, also creates difficulties for democratic struggle. To say that a political movement is always a movement that displaces the given boundaries, that extracts the specifically democratic, i.e., universalist, component of a particular conflict of interests in such and such a point of society, is also to say that it is always in danger of being confined to that conflict, in danger of ending up being no more than a defence of particular group interests in always singular struggles. This ever-present fact is even greater when it is the oligarchy that has the initiative of the confrontation, when the confrontation is led under the double face of the sovereign State and the 'powerless' State, especially as it now has on its side the historical necessity that yesterday gave dispersed struggles a horizon of common hope. One can always argue about the legitimacy of such and such a struggle, yet on each occasion one discovers the difficulty involved in linking this legitimacy to that of other combats, of constructing a democratic space in which they could converge in meaning and action. Those who fight to retain a public service, a system of labour laws, an unemployment benefits scheme, or a pension scheme, will always be accused, even if their struggle exceeds their particular interests, of leading a fight confined to the boundaries of national space, and of strengthening the State in requesting its enclosure be maintained. Conversely, those who proclaim that, from now on, democratic movement takes place beyond this framework, and oppose to these struggles of self-preservation the transnational affirmation of nomadic multitudes, will end up campaigning for the constitution of those very interstate institutions wherein the alliance of State oligarchs and financial oligarchs is assured.

Both the oligarchy's quandaries and democracy's difficulties can help us to understand the intellectual manifestations of antidemocratic fury. This fury is particularly intense in France, where a self-proclaimed group of intellectuals has a place in the media that gives it a power quite unheard-of in other countries in the day to day interpretation of contemporary phenomena and the formation of dominant opinion. We know just how this power was confirmed after 1968, when the milieus that manage opinion, shaken by a movement the comprehension of which exceeded the intellectual tools at their disposal, went on a feverish quest for interpreters of what had happened in the puzzling novelty of the times and the obscure depths of society.[52] The coming to power of the Socialists in 1981 gave these interpreters even more weight in the forming of public opinion, though the ambitions of some were not to be contented merely with the number of places on offer, and others never saw the interest the government professed to have in their ideas translated into concrete measures. This group today remains firmly in place; it is integrated into the managing of dominant opinion, and omnipresent in the media, though without any influence on the government's decisions – showered with benefits, it is humiliated in its aims, be they noble or base.

Some of them make the best of this supplementary function. Regularly called upon to explain to the public what is happening and what to think about it, they bring their science to shaping the prevailing intellectual consensus. They do it all the more smugly as they do not have to revoke either their science or their progressive convictions. The key idea of the consensus is in effect that global economic development attests to an historical necessity that we will just have to get used to, and that the only ones who can deny this necessity are the representatives of archaic interests and obsolete ideologies. And indeed, it is also this idea on which their conviction and their science is based. They believe in progress. They had faith in the progress of history when it was supposed to lead to socialist world revolution. They still believe in it now that it leads to the global triumph of the market. It is not their fault if history was mistaken. Consequently, they can unperturbedly reapply yesterday's lessons to today's conditions. To prove that the movement of things is rational, that progress is progressive, and that only the backward oppose it; and to show that in return the march forward does not stop relegating to the past the backward who retard the march forward – these basic principles of Marxist historical explanation also marvellously apply to the difficulties of 'modernization'. They legitimized the support a large fraction of intellectual opinion gave to the Juppé Government during the strikes of 1995, and have since unfailingly given credence to the denunciation of those archaic privileges that hold back that inevitable modernization, which itself never ceases producing new archaisms. The principal concept that animates this condemnation, that of populism, is itself borrowed from the Leninist arsenal. It enables that every movement against this depoliticization undertaken in the name of historical necessity be interpreted as a manifestation of a backward section of the population, or as an outmoded ideology. But the more backward people there are, the more need there is for the advanced to explain their backwardness. Progressives feel this solidarity and it tempers their antidemocratic stance.

Others cope less well with this position. The progressive faith is too naïve for them and the consensus too rosy. They also learnt their first lessons from Marxism. But their Marxism was not that of faith in history and the development of productive forces. Theoretically speaking, it was that of the critique that reveals the flipside of things – the truth of the structure under the surface of ideology, or that of exploitation under the appearance of rights and democracy. Practically speaking, it was a Marxism of classes and worlds in opposition, and of the rupture that breaks history in two. These people thus find it harder to cope with the fact that Marxism disappointed their expectations, and that history, the bad one, that which is never interrupted, has now enforced its reign. Regarding all this, regarding those years around '68 that saw the last great eruption in the West, their enthusiasm has transformed into *ressentiment*. They have not for all that given up on the things that form their triple inspiration: reading signs, denunciation, and rupture. Simply, they have shifted the target of condemnation, and changed temporal rupture. In a sense they are still subjecting the same thing to critique: for what is the reign of consumerism, if not the reign of commodities? And the principle of limitlessness, is it not that of capitalism? But the *ressentiment* puts the machine into reverse gear, inverting the logic of cause and effect. Formerly, it was a global system of domination that explained individual behaviour. The good souls then felt pity for the proletariat which, having let itself be taken in by the enticements offered by the betting office and household appliances, was regarded as the victim of a system that exploited it at the same time as nourishing its dreams. But as soon as the Marxist rupture failed to accomplish what the denunciation required, the denunciation was turned round: the individuals are not victims of a system of global domination. They are the ones responsible for it, the ones who impose the 'democratic tyranny' of consumption. The laws of capitalist accumulation, and the type of production and circulation of commodities they require, have become the simple consequence of the vices of those who consume these commodities, and especially of those who have the least means to consume. It is because democratic man is a being of excesses, an insatiable devourer of commodities, human rights and televisual spectacles, that the capitalist law of profit rules the planet. It is true that the new prophets do not complain about this reign. They do not complain either about financial oligarchies or about State oligarchies. They complain first about those who condemn them. It is not hard to understand why: denouncing an economic or State system means calling for systemic transformation. But who is it that is likely to make such demands for transformation if not those democratic men who blame these systems for not providing them with enough to satisfy their appetites? We must, then, take this logic to its conclusion. Not only are the vices of the system the vices of the individuals whose lives it governs. But the people most guilty, the exemplary representatives of this vice, are those who want to change the system, those who spread the illusion that it can be transformed so they can further indulge in their vices. The insatiable democratic consumer par excellence is the one who is opposed to the rule of State and financial oligarchies. We can easily see here the major argument through which May '68 was reinterpreted, the argument constantly repeated by historians and sociologists, and lengthily illustrated by bestselling novelists: the movement of '68 was only a movement of youth eager for sexual liberation and new ways of living. And as neither youth nor the desire for liberty by definition know what they want or what they are doing, these youth ended up bringing about the contrary of what they were proclaiming but the truth of what they sought: both a rejuvenation of capitalism and the destruction of all the familial, educational and other structures that stood in the way of the unlimited reign of the market that was penetrating ever deeper into the hearts and minds of individuals.

With politics forgotten, the word democracy thereby becomes both a euphemism designating a system that one no longer wants to call by its name, and the name of the diabolical subject that appears in place of that effaced word: a composite subject where the individual subjected to this system of domination and the one that denounces it are amalgamated. To paint a robotic portrait of democratic man, the best thing to do is to combine these characteristics: the young, idiotic consumer of popcorn, reality TV, safe sex, social security, the right to difference, and anticapitalist or 'alterglobalist' illusions. Thanks to him, the denouncers have what they need: the absolute culprit of an irremediable evil. Not a small culprit but a great culprit, one that brings about not simply the empire of the market that the denouncers make work for them, but also the ruin of civilization and humanity.

The reign of the imprecators thus establishes itself in amalgamating the new forms of commodity advertising, the demonstrations of those who are opposed to its laws, the half-heartedness of 'respect for difference', and the new forms of racial hatred, religious fanaticism and loss of the sacred. Everything and its contrary become the inevitable manifestation of the democratic individual that is dragging humanity to its ruin, a ruin that the imprecators deplore but that they would deplore even more were it not there to deplore. Of this evil individual one says both that he drags the civilization of the Enlightenment to its grave and that he pursues its deadly

works, that he is communitarian and without community, that
he has lost the sense of family values and the sense of their
transgression, the sense of the sacred and that of sacrilege.
Thereby one repaints old edifying themes in the sulphurous
colours of hell and blasphemy – man cannot do without God,
liberty is not licence, peace enfeebles the character, the desire
for justice leads to terror. Some call in the name of de Sade for
a return to Christian values; others marry Nietzsche, Léon
Bloy and Guy Debord to defend in a punk mode the positions
of the American evangelists; the worshippers of Céline put
themselves at the head of the hunt for anti-Semites, by which
they understand simply those who do not think like they do.

Certain imprecators satisfy themselves with having the
reputation of bitter clarity and indomitable solitude that is
gained by rehearsing in chorus the refrain of the 'crimes
against thought committed on a daily basis'[53] by the petty
man or the petty woman eager for petty enjoyment. For others
these sins are still too petty a thing with which to charge
democracy. They require a real crime to attribute to it, or
rather a sole crime, the absolute crime. So, they require a real
rupture in the course of history, that is to say a meaning of
history, a destiny of modernity that would be realized in the
rupture. This is why, at the moment the Soviet system was
collapsing, the extermination of the European Jews came to fill
the role of the social revolution as the event that cut the history
of the world in two. But to be able to fulfil that role, the real
authors of the crime had to have their responsibility taken
away from them. There is indeed the paradox: for anybody
wanting to make the extermination of the European Jews the
central event of modern history, Nazi ideology is not a
sufficient reason, because it is a reactive ideology, one which
was opposed to what at the time seemed to typify the modern

movement of history – the rationality of the Enlightenment, human rights, democracy and socialism. Ernst Nolte's thesis which turns the Nazi genocide into a defensive reaction to the genocide of the Gulag, itself alleged to be heir to democratic catastrophe, does not resolve the problem. The imprecators strive in effect to connect directly four terms: Nazism, democracy, modernity and genocide. But making Nazism into the direct realization of democracy is a tricky thing to demonstrate, even by means of the old counter-revolutionary argument which identifies 'Protestant individualism' as the root cause of democracy, and therefore of totalitarian terrorism. And making the gas chambers into the embodiment of the essence of technology that Heidegger designated as the fatal destiny of modernity is all that is needed to put Heidegger on the 'good' side, but is not enough to resolve the problem: modern and rational means can be perfectly well utilized in the service of archaic fanaticisms. If the reasoning is to function, a radical solution is required: eliminate the term that precludes the pieces from fitting together, that is, quite simply, Nazism. At the end of the process, then, this latter becomes the invisible hand that works toward helping democratic humanity triumph by getting rid of its intimate enemy, the people true to the law of kinship, so it can realize its dream: artificial procreation in the service of a desexualized humanity. From current research on embryos one retrospectively deduces the reason for the extermination of the Jews. From that extermination one infers that everything tied to the name democracy is merely the endless perpetuation of one and the same crime.

It is true that denouncing democracy as the interminable crime against humanity has no particularly widespread consequences. Those who dream of restoring a government of elites in the shadows of a rediscovered transcendence are perfectly happy with the current state of things in 'democracies'. And as they take the 'petty people', who contest this state of things, as their principal target, their imprecations ultimately unite with the admonitions of the progressives to come in support of the managerial oligarchs grappling with the rebellious moods of these petty people who, just like the asses and horses obstructing the streets in Plato's democratic city, obstruct the path of progress. As radical as they try to be in their dissensus, as apocalyptic as may be their discourse, the imprecators obey the logic of the consensual order: the logic that makes the signifier democracy into an indistinct notion lumping together into a single whole a type of state order and a form of social life, a set of ways of being and a system of values. Even if it means taking the ambivalence that feeds the official discourse to its extreme, and supporting, in the name of democratic civilization, the military campaigns of the evangelist plutocracy, which they stand alongside in denouncing the democratic corruption of civilization. The antidemocratic discourse of today's intellectuals adds the finishing touches to the consensual forgetting of democracy that both state and economic oligarchies strive toward.

In a sense, then, the new hatred of democracy is only one of the forms of confusion affecting this term. It doubles the consensual confusion in making the word 'democracy' an ideological operator that depoliticizes the questions of public life by turning them into 'societal phenomena', all the while denying the forms of domination that structure society. It masks the domination of State oligarchies by identifying democracy with a form of society, and it masks that of the economic oligarchies by assimilating their empire to the mere appetites of 'democratic individuals'. Hence, it can, in all seriousness, attribute all the phenomena connected with heightening inequality to the fateful and irreversible triumph of the 'equality of conditions', and so provide the oligarchic enterprise with its ideological point of honour: it is imperative to struggle against democracy, because democracy is tantamount to totalitarianism.

But the confusion does not simply lie in an illegitimate use of words that it would suffice to rectify. If words serve to blur things, it is because the conflict over words is inseparable from the battle over things. The word democracy was not forged by some expert concerned with identifying objective criteria by which to classify forms of government and types of society. On the contrary, it was invented as a term to 'indistinguish' things, to show that the power of an assembly of equal men could be nothing but the confusion of a formless and squawking horde, that this latter was to the social order what chaos was to the natural order. To understand what democracy means is to hear the struggle that is at stake in the word: not simply the tones of anger and scorn with which it can be imbued but, more profoundly the slippages and reversals of meaning that it authorizes, or that one authorizes oneself to make with regard to it. When, in the middle of the manifestations of heightening inequality, our intellectuals become indignant about the havoc wreaked by equality, they exploit a trick that is not new. Already in the nineteenth century, whether under the *monarchie censitaire* or under the authoritarian Empire, the elites of official France – of France reduced to two hundred thousand men, or subject to laws and decrees restricting individual and public liberties – were alarmed at the 'democratic torrent' that prevailed in society. Banned in public life, they saw democracy triumphing in cheap fabrics, public transport, boating, open-air painting, the new behaviour of young women, and the new turns of phrase of writers.[54] However, they were not innovative in this regard either. The pairing of democracy viewed both as a rigid form of government and as a permissive form of society is the original mode in which the hatred of democracy was rationalized by Plato himself.

This rationalization, as we saw, is not the simple expression of an aristocratic mood. It serves to ward off an anarchy or an 'indistinction' more formidable than that of streets encumbered by insolent children or stubborn asses: the primary indistinction between governors and governed, one which becomes evident when the obviousness of the natural power of the best or of the highborn is stripped of its prestige – the absence of a specific title to govern politically over those assembled other than the absence of title. Democracy is first this paradoxical condition of politics, the point where every legitimization is confronted with its ultimate lack of legitimacy, confronted with the egalitarian contingency that underpins the inegalitarian contingency itself.

That is why democracy shall never stop provoking hatred. It is also why this hatred is always present in disguise: in laughing tones against asses and horses in Plato's time; in furious diatribes against Benetton campaigns and episodes of *Loft Story* in the time of a worn-out French Fifth Republic. Whether these masks are amusing or scathing, the hatred underneath them has a more serious aim. It aims at the intolerable egalitarian condition of inequality itself. So we can reassure the sociologists, both professional and occasional, who declaim the worrying situation wherein democracy is now deprived of enemies.[55] Democracy is not about to have to brave the anguish of such a comfort. The 'government of anybody and everybody' is bound to attract the hatred of all those who are entitled to govern men by their birth, wealth, or science. Today it is bound to attract this hatred more radically than ever, since the social power of wealth no longer tolerates any restrictions on its limitless growth, and each day its mechanisms become more closely articulated to those of State action. The pseudo-European Constitution testifies to it a contrario: we are no longer in an age of expert juridical constructions designed to inscribe the irreducible 'power of the people' in oligarchic constitutions. This figure of the political and of political science is behind us. State power and the power of wealth tendentially unite in a sole expert management of monetary and population flows. Together they combine their efforts to reduce the spaces of politics. But reducing these spaces, effacing the intolerable and indispensable foundation of the political in the 'government of anybody and everybody', means opening up another battlefield, it means witnessing the resurgence of a new, radicalized figure of the power of birth and kinship. No longer the power of former monarchies and aristocrats, but that of the peoples of God. This power may openly assert itself in the terror practised by a radical Islam against democracy identified with States of oligarchic law. It may also bolster the oligarchic State at war with this terror in the name of a democracy assimilated, by American evangelists, to the liberty of fathers obeying the commandments of the Bible and armed for the protection of their property. In France, it can be invoked against democratic perversion to safeguard the principle of kinship, a principle that some leave in an indeterminate generality, but others unceremoniously identify with the law of the people instructed by Moses in the word of God.

Destruction of democracy in the name of the Koran; bellicose expansion of democracy identified with the implementation of the Decalogue; hatred of democracy assimilated to the murder of the divine pastor – all these contemporary figures have at least one merit. Through the hatred that they manifest against democracy, and in its name, and through the amalgamations to which they subject its notion, they oblige us to rediscover the singular power that is specific to it. Democracy is neither a form of government that enables oligarchies to rule in the name of the people, nor is it a form of society that governs the power of commodities. It is the action that constantly wrests the monopoly of public life from oligarchic governments, and the omnipotence over lives from the power of wealth. It is the power that, today more than ever, has to struggle against the confusion of these powers, rolled into one and the same law of domination. Rediscovering the singularity of democracy means also being aware of its solitude. Demands for democracy were for a long time carried or concealed by the idea of a new society, the elements of which were allegedly being formed in the very heart of contemporary society. That is what 'socialism' designated: a vision of history according to which the capitalist forms of production and exchange constituted the material conditions for an egalitarian society and its worldwide expansion. It is this vision that even today sustains the hope of a communism or a democracy of the multitude: the notion that the increasingly immaterial forms of capitalist production concentrated in the universe of communication are, from this moment on, to have formed a nomadic population of 'producers' of a new type; to have constituted a collective intelligence, a collective power of thought, affects and movements of bodies that is liable to explode apart the barriers of the Empire.[56] Understanding what democracy means is to renounce this faith. The collective intelligence produced by a system of domination is only ever the intelligence of that system. Unequal society does not carry any equal society in its womb. Rather, egalitarian society is only ever the set of egalitarian relations that are traced here and now through singular and precarious acts. Democracy is as bare in its relation to the power of wealth as it is to the power of kinship that today comes to assist and to rival it. It is not based on any nature of things nor guaranteed by any institutional form. It is not borne along by any historical necessity and does not bear any. It is only entrusted to the constancy of its specific acts. This can provoke fear, and so hatred, among those who are used to exercising the magisterium of thought. But among those who know how to share with anybody and everybody the equal power of intelligence, it can conversely inspire courage, and hence joy.

Notes

1. In 2004 a young French woman alleged she had been brutalized by a group of youths of North African origin on a Parisian train. The story was aired on France's evening television news bulletins and became a national *cause célèbre* until it became clear that she had only made up the story to get on television. *Translator's note*.
2. In early 2001, the director of the École de-s Science-s Politiques, Richard Descoings, amid much controversy, set up an alternative access scheme for students from disadvantaged backgrounds. *Translator's note*.
3. *The Economist*, 5 March, 2005.
4. Michel Crozier, Samuel P. Huntington, Joji Watanuki, *The Crisis of Democracy: Report on the Governability of Democracies to the Trilateral Commission*, New York University Press, 1975. Set up in 1973, the Trilateral Commission is a sort of club of reflection gathering together State officials, experts and businessmen from the United States, western Europe and Japan. It is often credited with having elaborated the ideas of the future 'New World Order'.
5. Aristotle, the *Constitution of Athens*, ch. XVI.
6. A student of Louis Althusser's at the École Normale Supérieure in the 1960s, Jean-Claude Milner was part of the Lacanian *Cahiers pour l'analyse*, which he co-founded in 1966. He is also a well-known linguist, the author of many books, and a former director of the Collège International de Philosophie in Paris. *Translator's note*.
7. For this the reader should consult Jean-Claude Milner's major work *Les Noms indistincts*, Seuil, 1983.

8. Samuel P. Huntington, *The Clash of Civilizations and the Remaking of World Order*, Simon and Schuster, 1996.

9. Cf. Claude Lefort, *The Democratic Invention: the Limits of Totalitarian Domination*, Johns Hopkins University Press, 2000 [1981].

10. Augustin Cochin, *Les Sociétés de pensée et la démocratie moderne*, Copernic, 1978. Augustin Cochin (1876–1916) was the son of baron Denys Cochin, who was a royalist deputy and minister during the First World War. As an avowed monarchist, Augustin Cochin collaborated on *Action française's* journal *Revue grise*. He died in battle in 1916. *Translator's note.*

11. Cf. Giorgio Agamben, *Homo Sacer: Sovereign Power and Bare Life*, trans. Daniel Heller-Roazen, Stanford University Press, 1998, and J. Rancière, 'Who Is the Subject of the Rights of Man?', *South Atlantic Quarterly*, 103, 2/3, Spring/Summer, 2004.

12. Dominique Schnapper, *Providential Democracy: an Essay on Contemporary Equality*, trans. John Taylor, Transaction, 2006 [2002], p. 124.

13. Ibid

14. On the various and sometimes contorted paths leading to contemporary neo-Tocquevillism, and notably on the conversion of the traditionalist, Catholic interpretation of Tocqueville into a postmodern sociology of 'consumer society', see Serge Audier, *Tocqueville Retrouvé: genèse et enjeux du renouveau tocquevillien français*, Vrin, 2004.

15. Daniel Bell, *The Cultural Contradictions of Capitalism,* Harper Collins, 1976. It must be noted that Daniel Bell's account still articulated a call for a return to puritanical values together with a concern for social justice, something which has completely disappeared with those who have revived his problematic in France.

16. Gilles Lipovetsky, *L'Ère du vide: essais sur l'individualisme contemporain*, Gallimard, 1983, pp. 145–146.

17. Jean Baudrillard, *The Consumer Society: Myths and Structures*, trans. Chris Turner, Sage, 1998 [1970], p. 50.

18. The movement of 1995 was a response to government plans to introduce a series of measures designed to bring France in line with international finance and move it toward an American-style system of pensions. In reaction to this popular movement, the editors of the journal *Esprit* published a petition in *Le Monde*, (9 December, 1995) supporting the government's 'audacious' plans and condemning the 'corporatist interests' of the workers. *Translator's note.*

19. Jules Ferry (1832–1893) became the French Minister of Education (*ministre d'Instruction publique*) in 1879. His aim was to build a secular and republican France on the basis of the school. *Translator's note.*

20. Renan's thesis is summed up in *La Réforme intellectuelle et morale, oeuvres complètes*, vol. 1, Calmann-Lévy, 1947, pp. 325–546. That in Renan's work this thesis goes hand-in-hand with a palpable nostalgia for the medieval Catholic people, putting its work and its faith at the service of the great cathedral works, is not a contradiction. Simply, the elites are

'Protestant', that is, enlightened and individualist, and the people 'Catholic', that is monolithic, and more believing than knowing. From Guizot to Taine and Renan, this is the kernel of the thinking of the elites in the nineteenth century.

21. Jean-Louis Thiriet, 'L'École malade de l'égalité', *Le Débat*, no. 92, Nov/ Dec, 1996.

22. For the development of these themes, the interested reader can consult the complete works of Alain Finkielkraut, notably *L'Imparfait du présent*, Gallimard, 2002, or, more economically, the interview of the same author by Marcel Gauchet, 'Malaise dans la démocratie: L'école, la culture, l'individualisme', *Le Débat*, no. 51, Sept/Oct, 1988. For a trendier version in a neo-Catholic punk style see the complete works of Maurice Dantec. Alain Finkielkraut teaches at the École Polytechnique in Paris. He is among France's cohort of public intellectuals who appear regularly on talk shows. Intellectually, he claims affiliation to the thought of Hannah Arendt and Emmanuel Lévinas. He has gained a certain notoriety for his controversial views concerning, for example, the riots in the Parisian *banlieues* and throughout France in 2005, which he attributed not to sociopolitical causes but to racial-ethnic ones, i.e. to the presence of Islamists. Maurice Dantec is a bestselling French cyberpunk fiction writer. Fleeing the 'Islamisation of France', he moved to Montreal, Canada, where, amongst other things, he collaborates with a conservative Francophone journal called *Égards*. Avowedly pro-Israel and pro-NATO, he endorses a 'Christian-Futurist' vision, which he pursues in his war against the contemporary nihilism he alleges is embodied in French leftism, the conservative right of Jacques Chirac, and of course the Islamists. *Translator's note.*

23. Finkielkraut, *L'Imparfait du présent*, p. 164.

24. Ibid., p. 200.

25. Jean-Jacques Delfour, '*Loft Story*: une machine totalitaire', *Le Monde*, 19 May, 2001. On the same theme – and in the same tone – see Damien Le Guay, *L'Empire de la télé-réalité: ou comment accroître le 'temps de cerveau humain disponible'*, Presses de la Renaissance, 2005. *Loft Story* is the French equivalent of the British *Big Brother* reality show. *Translator's note.*

26. Lucien Karpik, 'Being a victim; that means finding someone to blame', accounts collected by Cécile Prieur, *Le Monde*, 22–23 August, 2004. We know how important denouncing democratic tyranny is for the prevailing opinion. On this matter see notably Gilles William Goldnadel, *Les Martyrocrates: dérives et impostures de l'idéologie victimaire*, Plon, 2004.

27. In 1815, the Bourbon Restoration restricted the franchise to those able to afford a *cens* (fee) of 300 francs. *Un censitaire* is used in the sense of an elector able to pay the *cens*. *Translator's note.*

28. From this point of view one would benefit from reading *Le Salaire de l'idéal: la théorie des classes et de la culture au xxe siècle* (Seuil, 1997), in which the same Jean-Claude Milner analyzes, in the Marxist terms of the

unfortunate destiny of 'salaried bourgeoisie' become irrelevant to capitalist expansion, the processes attributed here to the fatal development of democratic limitlessness.

29. Jean-Claude Milner, *Les Penchants criminels de l'Europe démocratique*, Verdier, 2003, p. 32. I thank Milner for his responses to the comments I addressed to him about the theses presented in this book.

30. Benny Lévy, *Le Meurtre du pasteur: critique de la vision politique du monde*, Grasset Verdier, 2002. Benny Lévy (1945–2003), former secretary to Jean-Paul Sartre and head of the *Gauche prolétarienne*, was a former student of Louis Althusser. In 1978 he discovered Lévinas and soon became a fervent Talmudist. In 2002 he co-founded the Lévinas Institute in Jerusalem with Bernard-Henri Lévy and Alain Finkielkraut. *Translator's note.*

31. Lévy, *Le Meurtre du pasteur*, p. 313.

32. *Republic*, VIII, 562d–563d.

33. *Laws*, III, 690a–690c.

34. This was demonstrated when, under one of the Socialist Party governments, it was proposed that the members of the university selection committees be drawn by lot. No practical argument could be opposed to this measure. The situation consisted in a limited population composed by definition of individuals of equal scientific capacity. A single capability was thereby undermined: the inegalitarian competence, the skill of manoeuvring in the service of pressure groups; in other words, the attempt was doomed.

35. On this point see Bernard Manin, *The Principles of Representative Government*, Cambridge University Press, 1997 [1996].

36. Milner, *Les Penchants criminels*, p. 81.

37. Cf. J. Rancière, *Dis-agreement: Politics and Philosophy*, trans. Julie Rose, Minnesota University Press, 1999 [1995].

38. Cited by Pierre Rosanvallon, *Le Sacre du citoyen: histoire du suffrage universel en France*, Gallimard, 1992, p. 281.

39. Hannah Arendt, *On Revolution*, Viking, 1963, pp. 270–271.

40. On this point, see Rosanvallon, *Le Sacre du citoyen*, and Manin, *Principles of Representative Government*.

41. Democracy, said John Adams, signifies nothing other than 'the notion of a people that has no government at all' cited in Bertlinde Laniel, *Le Mot Democracy aux États-Unis de 1780 à 1856*, Presses Universitaires de Saint-Étienne, 1995, p. 65.

42. The *régime censitaire* spanned the years 1815 to 1848. *Translator's note.*

43. On the racial legislation of the Southern States, the reader can consult Pauli Murray, ed., *States' Laws on Race and Color*, Georgia University Press, 1997 [1951]. To those who constantly raise the spectre of 'communitarianism', this reading will give a somewhat more precise idea as to what protecting a communitarian identity can really mean.

44. See Paul Robiquet, ed., *Discours et opinions de Jules Ferry*, A. Colin, 1893–1898, volumes III and IV of which are devoted to the education laws. In his intervention at *La Cérémonie de la Sorbonne en l'honneur de Jules Ferry*

du 20 décembre 1905, Ferdinand Buisson underscores the pedagogical radicalism of the moderate Ferry in citing notably his address to the *Congrès pédagogique* on 19 April, 1881: 'Henceforth between secondary and primary education there shall no longer be any insurmountable abyss neither when it comes to methods nor when it comes to personnel.' However, one will note that the 'republican' campaign of the 1980s, without deigning to examine their competences, denounced the infiltration in colleges by primary teachers, those 'teachers of general education', and deplored the 'primarization' of secondary school teaching.

45. Cf. Alfred Fouillée, *Les Études classiques et la démocratie,* A. Colin, 1898. To gauge the importance of a figure like Fouillée at the time, it must be remembered that his wife was the author of a bestseller of republican pedagogical literature, *Le Tour de France de deux enfants.*

46. Fouillée, *La Démocratie politique et sociale en France,* F. Alcan, 1910, pp. 131–132.

47. Raymond Aron, *Democracy and Totalitarianism,* trans. Valence Ionescu, Weidenfeld and Nicolson, 1968, p. 83.

48. The École nationale d'administration, ENA, is one of the *Grandes Écoles,* the collective name for the leading tertiary education institutions in France outside of the university system. Graduates of the *Grandes Écoles* provide most ministers for governments of all persuasions and represent a large proportion of the upper echelons of the public service. *Translator's note.*

49. The referendum in France to ratify the proposed European Constitutional Treaty was held on 29 May, 2005. Voter turnout was 69%, of which 55% voted 'no'. *Translator's note.*

50. The word 'liberalism' lends itself today to all sorts of confusions. The European left use it in order to avoid the taboo word of capitalism. The European right use it to designate a vision of the world where the free market and democracy go hand-in-hand. The American evangelist right, for whom a *liberal* is a leftist destroyer of religion, family and society, remind us opportunely that these two things are quite different. The weight of a 'communist' China in the free market and in the financing of American debt, advantageously combining as it does the advantages of liberty and those of its absence, testifies to this in another manner. [The French term *libéralisme* can refer both to political liberalism and to economic neoliberalism. *Translator's note.*]

51. Cf. Linda Weiss, *The Myth of the Powerless State: Governing the Economy in a Global Era,* Polity, 1978.

52. On the emergence of this figure and its novelty with respect to the traditional figure of the intellectual spokesperson of the universal and the oppressed see D. and J. Rancière, 'La Légende des intellectuels', in J. Rancière, *Les Scènes du peuple,* Horlieu, 2003.

53. Maurice Dantec, *Le Théâtre des opérations: journal métaphysique et polémique 1999* and *Laboratoire de catastrophe générale. journal métaphysique et polémique 2000–2001,* Gallimard, 2003, p. 195.

54. For a good anthology of these themes see Hippolyte Adolphe Taine, *Vie et*

opinions de Frédéric Thomas Graindorge, Hachette, 1867. On 'democracy in literature', see the critique of *Madame Bovary* by Armand de Pontmartin in *Nouvelles Causeries du samedi*, Michel Very, 1860.

55. Cf. Ulrich Beck, *Democracy Without Enemies*, trans. Mark Ritter, Polity, 1998, and Pascal Bruckner, *La Mélancolie démocratique: comment vivre sans ennemis?*, Seuil, 1992.

56. Cf. Michael Hardt and Antonio Negri, *Empire*, Harvard University Press, 2001, and *Multitude: War and Democracy in the Age of Empire*, Penguin, 2005.

Index